Praise from around the world for

The Natural Laws of Selling

I have worked with Dan several times in the past and what has always impressed me is that he doesn't employ a "boxed" approach. Rather, he brings focus to the human/people aspect of the equation. By doing this he is able to achieve long-lasting results across the organization by understanding the dynamics, both inside and in front of your clients. Now, in his new book, "The Natural Laws of Selling," he expands on this concept and *brings to light the power of connecting techniques and methods to natural laws.* Brilliant! – Fred Beyerlein, Managing Director, FGB Technologies, LLC

* * *

Mr. Jacobs has a way of rephrasing basic truths that really penetrate through the mist of complexity found in many other books on sales, those that merely state aphorisms and without theoretical substance. The *direct, common sense approach found in* The Natural Laws Of Selling is truly a remarkable contribution to the field of selling. – Professor Cary Kilner, Ph.D. University of New Hampshire

* * *

This book is *in a class by itself.* The Natural Laws of Selling defines the quintessential essence of selling at all levels. Instead of offering simple sales tricks and tips, it cuts through to the core of selling and reveals what makes all sales tactics and strategies work, which is the missing ingredient in most sales efforts. We ordered copies of the book for everyone on our team. - Greg Marsden, Director of Marketing, LeadSmartMarketing.com

* * *

Dan's advice has been enormously valuable to me – especially in those complex situations where no obvious solution was identifiable. For example, after retooling the sales force, it *broke all previous company sales records*. His remarkable skills in sales management, motivation and training have made a lasting positive effect in my life. - Steve Vachss, Vice President, Presenternet.com

*　*　*

The Natural Laws Of Selling has accomplished something like no other book on the subject: *a new way of thinking about selling*. Mr. Jacobs' experience-based insight into sales technology shows you how to harness the power of natural laws to sell yourself, your products and services, and put you back in charge of your life. - Bob Lippmann, Owner, President, RSVP Orange County

*　*　*

"The Natural Laws of Selling" is a *one of a kind* reference and just may be a seminal event in the science of the sales process. It contains enlightening insights about people and new ideas about selling that will change the way people think about the profession. This book also reveals an understanding of the inner workings of the sales process and how it contributes to building successful relationships between people that is unprecedented. I am a big fan of this writing. - Professor Emeritus Billy Brown, Esq, Former Associate Dean of Business Programs and Director of MBA Program William Carey University

*　*　*

"The Natural Laws of Selling," is not just about selling things. It is about how to live your life and treat people with respect. It is a very easy read and is organized in a way you can pick it up at any point and find some sort of simple revelation that seems so profound and yet you haven't made that connection until you read it. – Geoff Winstead, Musician, Author

* * *

Cover to cover, this book is an amazing journey. You come away with the gestalt of sales in a way no other text has provided. Like all endeavors, successful selling is not a matter of amassing a bunch of tricks and methods; it is a complete state of mind. Better than any other book I've read on the subject, The Natural Laws of Selling helps establish this. - Duke Cullinan, writer

* * *

This book is not just for those who work as salesmen or women. The basic 'laws' he talks about are universal in relationships of any kind. - M. Warton, photographic artist

* * *

The book is like a *smack in the forehead*! The beauty of what Dan prescribes in "The Natural Laws of Selling" is the fact that the principles are simple. It really gets to the heart of the matter that selling, and business in general, is all about dealing with people. Actually, Dan is pulling one over on us by calling this a book about selling. What he is shining the light on in this book goes well beyond selling, and anyone, in any position, in any industry will benefit from what he discusses. With this book, mastery of selling really can become a reality. - Keith Melnick, President, KAYAK

* * *

The premise of this book is simple and straightforward: if you act in accordance with the natural laws of selling, you increase your personal power in all areas of your life. "The Natural Laws of Selling" reveals the secrets of how to harness the raw power of natural laws, stay out of trouble and jump-start any business with less stress. Who can argue with that? - Ron Morris, Founder and President FiftyX Consulting Business Service.

* * *

The Natural Laws of Selling is a *tour de force* in the area of selling and human relations. Reducing complexity to simple observable laws is no small feat. Dan has accomplished this with style and wisdom. The book is well designed and flows from one key topic to another. I've already used it in consulting with clients with excellent results.! – James N. Consultant, Advisor

* * *

It sent chills up my spine! And that was just from reading the overview of this book. I was involved in sales for years but I never did I codify and demystify the inner workings of the sales process as Daniel Jacobs has with this book. This book is a wake-up call for any salesperson. He has demystified of the sales process. It makes me excited about the possibilities for the future! – Angelyn Arcaro Romanow, Business Consultant

* * *

This book gives both novices and experts the tools to excel. There is admittedly a lot of psychology involved the selling process, which can be daunting. But this book cuts through to the heart of the inner game of selling with clear speaking, simple language and easy to understand concepts. Highly recommend for individuals in the sales field or anyone striving for success. – L. Theodore, Church Administrator

* * *

You know immediately when something rings true. This is a well written, easily understood work which points anyone involved in sales in the right direction. Review of the basics, even for a "pro," can act to allow for a re-evaluation of the importances connected with effective selling. - J. A., Director, AAS LLC

* * *

Well, this book doesn't give you any magic tricks or sleight of hand, but it does give you something far more valuable. It shows you the essential truths that take all the mystery of out of selling. There are no empty promises here. Combining The **Natural Laws of Selling** with a **disciplined practice of workable methods** will give you the stability, certainty and effortless competence that you've been looking for in your career. – Charles J., Web Designer and Internet Consultant

* * *

If only I had read even just the article on "assumptions" in this book BEFORE I made the decision to take a new job in another city. Yikes! I could have saved myself a lot of aggravation! Great book! – Commodore Perry Barrett, professional recording engineer

* * *

I really enjoy reading things that seem so obvious once I see it - yet - I never thought of it before. "The Natural Laws of Selling" is one of those books that make me nod my head and exhale slowly . . . (body language for "of course"). I am now half way through the book and have decided to buy a copy for each of my sales reps in Nashville. - Randy Vader, C.E.O. Praisegathering Music Group

* * *

It just makes sense! Finally, a book that tells it like it is, chocked full of common sense tips anyone can use. – C. Wilson, President, Executive Sales Consultant

THE NATURAL LAWS OF SELLING

The Essential Truths

Daniel Jacobs

Wright Road Publishing, 2014
Toluca Lake, California

Daniel Jacobs/Wright Road Publishing

10153 ½ Riverside Drive

Toluca Lake, CA 91602

www.wrightroadpublishing.com

The Natural Laws of Selling/The Essential Truths/Daniel Jacobs—1st edition

ISBN 978-0-99155-041-8

Dedicated to my Myrna Jacobs, my wife, my best friend, my love and the best person I will ever know. And to my grandson, Bryce Jacobs, who has a natural ability to connect with people and engender trust and affection.

Acknowledgements

To my wife, Myrna Jacobs, senior editor over the years it took to bring this book to fruition. The enormous value of her natural skills in communication and her instinctive understanding of human nature cannot be overstated. She has made this writing far better than it would have been otherwise. Without her support and unfailing encouragement, this book would not have seen the light of day.

The following people also contributed directly to making this project happen. Each one deserves my heartfelt thanks.

To Goeff Winstead, editor nonpareil. His experience, professionalism, and incomparable attention to small detail were indispensable in bringing this work to its final form.

To Sarah Jensen, editor, who did the first major edit and was an enormous help in refining the work.

To my children, Duke Cullinan, Lauren Wilson, and Evan Jacobs, whose unfailing encouragement was an ongoing source of reassurance that my work had real value and was worth pursuing.

To Duke Cullinan, in particular, who held the job of *on-call* writing consultant and occasional ghost writer, contributed enormously to improve the quality of the writing, especially in the early formative stages.

To Rod Jacobs, my brother, who did a masterful job of proofreading and editing on the print version of this book.

To Chuck Jacobs, musician, web designer and author, he developed the first website featuring my writings on selling and was a continuing source of encouragement and support for my work over the years required to bring this book to its present form.

To Lauralyn Theodore, my sister, who read the early versions and provided helpful suggestions and feedback.

To my long-time friend, Professor W. Cary Kilner, Ph.D., University of New Hampshire, who shares with me the love of words and grammar when used to enhance understanding of life. His advices, feedback, and suggestions during the writing of this material was priceless.

To Ron Morris, for his professionalism and creative imagination in the layout and design of the cover of this book.

To the authors of countless earlier books on sales and selling who paved the way. My hope is that this writing is a worthy addition to their work.

There are other individuals who contributed, directly or indirectly to bringing this book to completion. Their suggestions, encouragement and feedback have helped enormously.

Some of the names (in no particular order) are: Fred Beyerlein, Terry Puterbaugh, Bob Lippmann, Professor Emeritus Billy Brown, Esq., Angelyn Arcaro-Romanow, Dr. John Casillas, DVM, Debby Casillas, Gary Wattman, Chuck Jacobs, Curt Wilson, Wm. Newman, Kate Melnick, Keith Melnick, Ron Oates, Jack Kimmell, Ph.D., Lauralyn Theodore, J. Newell, S. Hawley, Richard Wetzel, Jerry Cameron, Greg Marsden, Mike McLeod, Keyanus Price, and Charles Rutherford, Ph.D., and Steve Vachss.

The list of names of those who have inspired me and helped me over the years is so long I'm sure I overlooked many, but you know who you are and I thank you.

Table of Contents

Forward

What Makes This Book Different?

There is nothing new about selling. Over the years, countless new methods of selling have been tried and either rejected as useless, or eventually accepted as workable. But the underlying principles and basic laws have not changed since time immemorial – all that has changed is the ways of applying them.

What makes this book different is that it brings to light *the power of connecting methods to the underlying principles* contained in the natural laws.

There is nothing mystical or mysterious about "The Natural Laws of Selling," except perhaps in the sense that these laws are unknown to most people; and those who have used these laws successfully appear to have some magical power. But, this is not magic. It is simply a common sense method of showing you how to empower your methods and techniques by hitching them to the natural laws.

The natural laws do exist. But, the complexity and mystery surrounding them has now been penetrated and clarified. Their power has been revitalized by identifying and discarding the false and failed assumptions of the past.

Here is what is different about this book: Using time-honored methods and techniques and combining them with the unchanging fundamental principles empowering all selling is the easiest and fastest way to achieve results that only dreams are made of.

As discussed in the book, the driving forces behind all selling techniques have been found to derive solely from the underlying natural laws. Once you learn to harness the raw power of the natural laws, then, seamlessly, your methods of selling begin to generate an intensity that is compellingly persuasive. And that is worth working for, isn't it?

1

Introduction

"Life is, indeed, terribly complicated – to a man who has lost his principles."

The words above, from G.K. Chesterton, one of the best writers and thinkers of the twentieth century, written over a century ago, are perhaps even more apropos in our world today.

Faced with the ever-increasing pace of changes in technology, avenues of communication, and methods of social interaction, life can look terribly complicated, indeed.

And as Chesterton said, life is all the more complicated when approached without principles. But it's not as if we aren't trying.

Perhaps trying a new method is easier to face than finding the real reason for poor results. So instead, we adopt the newest and latest selling technique to keep our spirits up, only to have our hopes dashed once again when these too provide less than satisfying results.

But the process of adding even more complexity to the mix—trying to learn and adopt one new method after another—is not the way out. What we should be doing is looking for a way to simplify things.

The thing is—selling is not that complex. It only seems that way when cluttered with odd opinions, false assumptions, and wrong ideas. And, of course, anything made too complicated to be understood won't be used.

This is a concept shared by Steve Jobs, co-founder and CEO of Apple, Inc., when he said in an interview with Business Week in 1998,

"That's one of my mantras – focus and simplicity. Simple can be harder than complex: You have to work hard to get your thinking clean to make it simple."

So, in search for a simpler, user-friendly solution to problems in selling –

one that didn't also create more problems – I went back to the essential truths and natural laws, found in the basics of all selling.

But what is a natural law anyway? The dictionary provides the answer in the definitions of these words:

Natural: Inherent; having a basis in nature, reality and truth; not made or caused by humankind.

Law: An existing condition, which is binding and immutable (cannot be changed).

Basically, natural law is the incremental acquisition of knowledge, gained through observation.

A natural law is something that you can think with and use. It aligns other observations and actions and allows you to predict consequences. It doesn't rely on belief, trust or opinion. All that is required is a willingness to observe and see for yourself.

Instead of searching endlessly for new methods to miraculously eliminate all selling problems, all that is required is to tap into the raw energy of these basic principles, which are after all, what give stability, strength and power to your methods.

The natural laws of selling are the driving force behind all methods of selling and their discovery has been called a seminal event in the profession. This introduces a whole new way of thinking about selling, one that is simple, focused, and more effective. By harnessing the power inherent in the natural laws of selling, your methods begin to generate an intensity that makes them compellingly persuasive.

The Natural Laws of Selling draws upon empirical, practical experience and direct observations of what works. Abstract, theoretical or hypothetical ideas without actual practical use were discarded, and instead, the focus was on what could be understood and applied in the real world.

This research ended up as a compilation of articles on my observations and discoveries *about people and about selling* (the two are inseparable), presented somewhat loosely in the order that they were written.

The book itself is unique in that it has been deliberately *designed for browsing*, inviting you to read any article at random. You will also find a few of the vital concepts touched on more than once, if only to underscore their importance.

As the overriding intention was that *quick study would pay off in fast results*, each article contains at least one essential truth about selling that can boost your spirits and your sales today. Additionally, acting in accordance with essential truths of natural laws will empower your abilities in all areas of life – but especially in selling. Because understanding the basic principles will allow you to evaluate your own methods and adjust or adapt as needed.

Finally, the evidence indisputably supports the fact that *understanding people* will fortify your understanding of selling. This alone can replace insecurity and doubt with confidence and certainty, leading inevitably to a mastery of the fundamentals, which is the route to excellence in selling.

CHAPTER 1

AND YOU CALL THIS A LIVING?

The clock said 4:30 AM, scolding me for still being awake.

I was stuck, once again, with that cold-sweat fixation that tomorrow could signal the end of my career. Try as I might, I couldn't escape those all-pervasive thoughts of worry and dread. And with my anxiety escalating by the minute, the chances of any sleep went from slim to none.

Others are out there, I thought, better prepared and more determined. And I'm so worn out, I'm running on the fumes of what empty used to smell like, stuck with the feeling that I'm going to blow another opportunity, one that I desperately need! The only thing I knew for sure was, *something had to change.*

* * *

Now, if this sounds all too familiar, you're not alone. In fact, you really *shouldn't even be surprised.* After all, when you've been thrown in over your head to do a job, for which you've had no effective training or practice, who would expect anything different? Absent any real familiarity in the basics of selling, who can blame you for wanting to quit?

Now, we all know that the *wrong thing to do is nothing.* But, where does that leave us?

Well, if you're still with me this far, there is hope, and it is because of these three important factors:

a) You feel that there may be *something to learn.*
b) You're serious enough about *changing your life.*
c) You're willing to *do something about it.*

* * *

This book has something for everyone, from beginners who want to get started on the right foot, to working sales professionals in the field who want to break through to the next plateau of sales results and stability.

Sales managers who need a resource for helping salespeople understand and apply the fundamentals of the subject quickly and efficiently will also find this text extremely useful.

Understanding the importance of the fundamental principles underlying all selling and aligning your methods to them may just change your career in magical and surprising ways.

For the power of *the natural laws of selling* combined with a disciplined practice of workable methods can give you the stability, certainty and effortless competence that you've been searching for.

So, let's get started.

HOW IT BEGAN

The approach to this book is not theoretical, but rather it is oriented toward action in real life – in your career.

Also, it doesn't require anything more from you than your natural curiosity to find a way to become better at what you're already doing.

My writing in this text had its humble beginnings as a series of weekly sales articles written for salespeople at an international marketing company where I was employed as a senior executive. The sales personnel of the company were already veteran professionals in their own right, and were very clear about what they needed from me.

They wanted plain-speaking articles on sales that *cut through the bull* and delivered a message that focused on selling in the real world, not on some untried theory.

They were also adamant about what they *didn't want.*

They definitely did not want an ivory tower, academic treatise full of graphs and numbers, or some hypothetical scheme of selling, or any other complicated, unworkable psychobabble.

They summarily rejected anything not based on *common sense application in the real world.* Happily, this was in line with the focus of all my writings so we were seeing eye-to-eye.

Soon, within the company, my writings became the *go-to resource* for everyday use by the salesmen and women in the company. Why? Because every article was chock-full of new discoveries based on basic selling principles, real-life experiences, reminders of what they already knew, plus new, relevant information for ready use in everyday selling activities.

It became clear that these writings were *a new way of thinking about selling.* These were fresh discoveries about the inner workings of the sales process not a rehash of past techniques and methods. The focus was tightened, complexities exposed and stripped away, *false assumptions* and unworkable fads were uncovered and discarded while searching for a solution where simplicity reigned supreme.

The universally workable laws were isolated and clarified and the time-proven basics were strengthened by understanding and applicability in the real world of sales.

Throughout, this single, straightforward purpose remained the guideline to this writing: **focus only on what worked** and discard the rest.

The value of this approach will be instantly evident in the change in your attitude and even further proved by the increase in sales results.

I consider it no accident that this book is now *in your hands.*

TEN UNIVERSAL PRINCIPLES

There are many more natural laws of selling than those included in this book, but to jump-start your understanding and use of the universal principles, I've included ten of them at the start that you can read and put to use today. Each of these is a natural law of selling.

1. You're not in the sales business; you're in the people business, helping the individual.

2. The most effective way to get people to trust you is to first trust yourself.

3. Two key factors in selling are making a friend before you make a sale and adding value to their lives.

4. Getting someone interested in you starts with being sincerely interested in them.

5. Selling is a process of finding commonality, building trust and agreement, enhancing understanding and adding value by fulfilling a need or satisfying a want.

6. What the customer is buying is always more important than what you're selling.

7. Forcing or bullying a prospect will always generate resistance.

8. Before you can turn prospect into a customer, they must see a personal benefit in what you're selling.

9. The core competency (stock in trade) of the professional salesperson is the tendering of helpful solutions by the artful use of communication skills.

10. All things being equal, people always prefer to do business with their friends.

Of course, there are an unlimited number of methods of applying these principles, but you should expect to see dramatic improvement in your results by understanding and practicing even one or two of the ten examples above.

COMMON DENOMINATORS OF SELLING

Common denominators are standards, beliefs, traits, attitudes, principles or the like, held in common and shared by all members of a group.

Every profession has common denominators, which are the bedrock basics requisite to success in that field, learned from hard-won experience in the trenches. Knowing and applying these principles and natural laws can make your job easier and far more effective.

Albert E. N. Gray, author of "The Common Denominator Of Success" had this to say about the subject:

"The common denominator of success – the secret of success of every man who has ever been successful – lies in the fact that he formed the habit of *doing things that failures don't like to do.*"

Whether you agree or not, the fact is, *if you make it a habit of avoiding* what needs to be done, you'll end up with undesirable results.

But, instead, if you *make a habit of being willing to do what needs to be done*, when it has to be done, you will begin to see consistently desirable results.

This is what differentiates the successful from those who are not.

Following some of the key common denominators will get you off on the right foot on the road to success in selling.

1. **Understanding** the basics of the profession. This means that excellence in selling comes from a mastery of the fundamentals not simply accumulating tricks and techniques.

2. **Familiarity** with the selling process - from initial contact through to final closing. This means practice of each separate step of the progression and not just focusing on one step (focusing only on closing the sale for example).

3. **Awareness** that you are always selling to an individual person. This means that you must be interested in the customer first and you second.

4. **Recognition** that forcing the customer creates sales resistance. Resorting to force exposes the fact that you have skipped a step in the process.

5. **Professionalism** is developed with consistent practice, correction, and refinement of the application of your tools.

6. **Appreciation** for the importance of initiative, self-discipline, persistence, patience and perseverance.

Mastering even one of these common denominators can dramatically increase your sales closing ratio, mastering them all will place you firmly on the road to success.

THE ELEPHANT IN THE ROOM

The elephant in the room is an idiomatic phrase for a problem so obvious it can't be ignored, but no one wants to discuss; preferring instead to pretend it's not there.

This situation is easy to recognize when you start hearing these ways of dealing with a problem: explanations, justifications, and reasons of why it's not a problem, dismissing it, neglecting it, running away, hiding, succumbing to it or kicking the can down the road so it doesn't have to be dealt with right now.

None of these *solutions* will solve the problem, but people use them all the time. They depend on luck or think it's just fate and they can do nothing about it.

There is also a natural law about all this that can't be ignored:

Law: Any problem not faced directly will intensify far out of proportion to the initial problem.

But even if you do face it directly, you're not out of the woods yet. This is only the first step. But at least you're heading in the right direction, as doing nothing is always the wrong thing to do.

Fear of making a mistake can paralyze you into inaction. Because the minute *you decide not to face* a problem, your attention gets even more stuck on what you're not facing – if only to remind you not to think about it – and you begin to form a *habit of not confronting*. Negative emotions follow with concern, anxiety, apprehension, unease, sleepless nights and free-floating anxiety filled days.

This is a trap. The unknown creates mystery, which creates concern, which creates worry, which creates stress in a vicious circle of inaction, uncertainty and confusion, all of which bar your inspection of what is really going on. Not a happy situation to be sure.

Seneca, the Greek philosopher, had a way of dealing with what he did not know. When asked if he was afraid of dying, he replied,

"Absolutely not, why should I be afraid of something I know nothing about."

It's a good point. Pick your battles. Simply refuse to be afraid of what you don't know and put your attention on what you do know.

This alone can free up your attention to look beyond the problem and examine possibilities otherwise unavailable to you.

Law: Any solution that can't be implemented is not one.

PRIMARY BARRIER

"With many companies trying to shake off the drag of a global recession, CEOs are eager to find growth. One place they need to look is in *their own sales organizations.*" - *Harvard Business Review* Blog, 2012.

We are indeed moving into *mare incognito* (unknown and uncharted seas) and are facing challenges far more uncertain than ever experienced. Witness the turbulent, roiling seas of the business community as proof positive.

Competition, domestically and internationally, is intense and growing; firms are merging, outsourcing, acquiring, and divesting faster than can be reported; emerging technology is replacing traditional methods at the speed of light; products are becoming more complex; customers are demanding better service, faster delivery and lower prices; the list goes on.

Navigating these waters in an increasingly volatile and unpredictable global environment is a key challenge facing all businesses.

And it seems clear that *few will survive without an effective sales force.*

To stay alive and expand in the 21st century firms must face this all-encompassing force that affects every aspect of business.

After all, trained and experienced salespeople may be the *last line of defense* for the consumer because they alone are uniquely experienced in *dealing with uncertainty* in the customer, or at least they should be.

Law: Uncertainty is a primary barrier to selling.

And this also implies uncertainty in both the salesperson and the customer. The pressure on salespeople to develop greater skills to meet the challenges of this brave new world is intense and cannot be ignored. But where can these skills be found?

The best way is to become securely grounded in the *basics of human interaction* (the key to all selling) and go back to mastering the basic fundamentals.

The little-known secret is that the basic laws of selling are no different than the common-sense methods of dealing with people. Learn them. Use them. Expand and prosper!

FOUR THINGS YOU NEED TO KNOW

Long ago, someone asked me to summarize what they needed to know to succeed in selling; and do it in four points! Well, it took some doing, but I did it.

Here they are, four *natural laws of selling* you need to know that I consider important to all sales activities.

Just show up

This is the first thing you need to know: just show up, physically and mentally prepared to do your best every time; no exceptions, no excuses.

It's been said that eighty percent of success is showing up and I agree, as everything stems from this basic concept.

Also, *you must decide* to show up and be there, and do it for yourself; no one can do it for you.

Selling is an *action* verb

The word itself implies *action*. In selling, if you don't have the intention and drive to *make something happen*, it won't happen.

Don't waste your time looking for excuses, justifications, or explanations of why the sale didn't go as expected. Either you *caused* the sale to happen or you didn't. Simply stated, *you're either looking for a reason to explain failure or you're looking for a way to make it happen*. This realization alone can be a game-changer.

People always buy a personal benefit

It's said that knowing *what* people buy can make you a living, but knowing *why* people buy can make you rich.

The question of why *people buy anything* prompted my writing this book in the first place, and the answer is always the same: *People buy what they consider to be a personal benefit.*

By isolating this simple, common sense basic you can adjust your sales procedure as necessary to ensure the desired result.

Selling is always about the people.

It's easy to assume you're in the sales business, but you're not.

You're in the *people business*, with a clear *focus on the individual* (not their job title or position).

This discovery was far and away the *most important* one of all, because all prospects, customers and clients are unique *individuals*. And they want to be treated as such. Keeping my attention on that specific person, adding value to their lives and giving good service makes all the difference. Nothing else even comes close, and it's something they never forget.

There are, of course, many more points that you need to know, but everything starts somewhere.

These four points are indispensable to have under your belt; and as they are the barebones rudimental basics that you cannot ignore, here they are once again:

1. Just show up.
2. Selling is an *action* verb.
3. People always buy a personal benefit.
4. Selling is always about the people.

HAD TOO MUCH TO THINK?

I'm always on the lookout for anecdotes to help explain ideas. This one came unexpectedly while my friend Terry Puterbaugh and I were enjoying a couple of good cigars and a rare scotch.

He casually asked, *"Why is it that my best golf of the year comes at the first two rounds?*

I offered, *"Could it be something about muscle memory taking over, without conscious thought?"*

He laughed out loud and said, "I think Captain Beefheart, got it right when he said, "I think people have had too much to think."

Note: "Captain Beefheart," was the stage name of Don Van Vliet, a unique imperious and uncompromising artist whose music was largely a cult obsession.

He went on to say, "I'm probably better off to just let my instincts take over and just concentrate on the experience I'm involved in at the moment."

At that moment, we both realized that *long thinking leaves you short on good experience and that* the less clutter you have between the **idea and the action,** the more you get done.

Of course, this aligns with another basic principle having to do with the shortest distance between A and B being a straight line. Even Sam Walton subscribed to this business philosophy expressed with his well-known theory of business, *"Ready, Fire, Aim."*

You may disagree with his mass merchandising approach to retailing, but you'll have to admit that he was extraordinarily successful in building Wal-Mart into a retail colossus. He was a pragmatist, not a perfectionist. He understood that any idea, project, or product has *time limitations.*

His philosophy was to get the project to market or to completion as quickly and as well done as possible, given the time constraints of the marketplace. Once it was up and running, a project could be adjusted and improved and the kinks ironed out.

The idea was simple and effective: Don't let *thinking supplant doing.*

I think he was on to something that we could all use to improve our sales results. It's clear that what separates the winners from the wannabe's is that they *focus on getting something done, not thinking about doing it.*

Moral: If you're not getting things done that should be, check and see if there is too much chatter and clutter in between the idea and the action. If so, *you just may have had too much to think.*

PRINCIPLES AND METHODS

The following quote by Ralph Waldo Emerson contains *everything you need to know* about avoiding trouble in your sales career, or your life.

"The man who grasps principles can successfully select his own methods. The man who tries methods, ignoring principles, is sure to have trouble."

Principles and methods are the *why and the how* behind everything you are doing in your profession. They comprise the essential underlying structure supporting every aspect of selling.

A principle is an immutable, natural law or essential truth, which, when followed, inevitably produces predictable results. It does not change because you lack the self-discipline to learn and use it.

A principle teaches you why to do something.

For example, once you become aware of the law of gravity, you know why it is in your best interests to follow that law or suffer the consequences.

A method is a way of learning *how to apply* that law and acquire skill in using it to your advantage.

Techniques and tactics of how to sell are as varied and individual as there are salesmen and women. There can be an infinite number of methods and ways to apply a fundamental principle while the basic law itself remains unchanged – and far more valuable.

Law: Methods teach you *how to apply* a principle. Principles show you *why it works.*

Any guarantee of success, in sales or in life, must contain both of these elements in proper balance to ensure longevity in your career. Luckily, the principles are easy to learn and apply. When this is accomplished, the methods make sense and are far more effective. Understand the principles and you can develop your own methods. Long-term success in selling depends on an understanding of basic principles and developing and practicing workable methods

ASSUMPTIONS CAN BE HAZARDOUS TO YOUR *WEALTH*

The strange thing about assumptions is that they are both an asset and a liability. However, if adopted without inspection, they can be extremely hazardous to your *wealth.*

We're told that an assumption is something taken for granted and believed true without proof. For example, even if our headlights only allow us to see about 100 feet ahead of us while driving at night, *we assume* that the road will continue in front of us.

We unconsciously trust that the road will be there as it always has been, and that our assumptions can be put on automatic without liability. They are valuable in that they allow us to predict a future without constant reevaluation of information. Most of the time, we're right. This is when an assumption is seen as an asset.

Physical universe assumptions, subject to inspection by direct observation in scientific manner are not the same as interaction and interpersonal relationships between human beings which are often less visible.

This fact is particularly true in the profession of selling where you discover very quickly that people can and do act and react in very unpredictable ways. To assume that they will act or react in a certain way because they have done so in the past will often leave you unsatisfied or worse.

This is when *assumptions become a liability.*

It is sound advice to avoid relying on assumptions or preconceived notions too heavily. We can assume that information is reliable, but should do more research to verify that the information is, in fact, accurate or trustworthy. It could be said that the only safe assumption is that your first assumptions could be false. This idea is particularly germane to the following quote.

"Believe only half of what you see and nothing that you hear." - Edgar Allen Poe.

Here is a typical assumption (also a natural law) for you to practice:

Law: People are motivated largely by self-interest.

How valuable is this assumption? Does it simplify your life or add further complexity? Does it allow you to predict things better with or without it? Have you ever directly observed this to be true?

Only you can answer the questions above. It is the process of observing, evaluating and making up your own mind that determines the value or importance of the assumption.

If you base your judgment on facts in evidence, this will deter you from adopting false assumptions without inspection. Here's another assumption. Test it out and see if it proves to hold any value for you or not:

Law: Market to people. Sell to the individual.

Ask yourself the same questions as in the first example.

How did you do? Again, there is no right answer unless you see it to be right for yourself (after observation, evaluation and decision).

By the way, you get very fast at this procedure after a few times, but take your time in the beginning and the process will sink in.

But let's look at these assumptions a little closer. As we learn from the theory of Ockham's Razor, selecting the hypothesis that makes the fewest assumptions is generally the fastest way to the truth.

Can you see that the assumptions, "people are motivated by self-interest" and "you're always selling to an individual," can help you understand the overall process of selling and get better results? If so, it becomes a workable assumption for you. And that is all we're going for, isn't it?

If you can see that an assumption works for you, then it has value and a personal benefit. But once an assumption, thought to be true, proves unworkable, you should challenge it as a *false assumption* and get rid of it.

Once tuned in to the concepts of assumptions (false or true), you'll see them in abundance in every day speech, thrown around like so much confetti on New Years Eve. You would be well served to train yourself to catch these false assumptions before it's too late.

Here is another observation regarding assumptions, specifically intended for salespeople who live and breathe by their communication skills.

Law: Miscommunications can often be traced back to *differing assumptions.*

If it is beginning to dawn on you that this could be the source of many of your thorny problems with others, *you are right.* In any case, assumptions are a good starting point for investigation and analysis for any difficult situation.

Once you discover that an assumption has *outlived its usefulness,* it should be tossed aside.

When things are not working as you've planned; when nothing seems to work out as intended; *seek out and discard any old assumptions or fixed solutions* that may be clouding your thoughts and actions.

For some reason, assumptions (including false assumptions) tend to flourish and grow in the sales profession, to the misfortune of many. In fact, there are likely as many assumptions, opinions, rigid ideas and bad habits as there are people working in the profession.

Fortunately, the principles of selling, such as truthfulness, trust, fairness, honesty, integrity, honor and fair dealing are *basic assumptions* that you can always count on. They are timeless and they are true.

To stay on top of your game, get in the habit of challenging your assumptions and adjust as necessary. And keep a *weather eye* (shrewd watchfulness and alertness) for those pesky unexamined *false assumptions.* You might just find things going a lot easier than you suspected.

ATTITUDE IS EVERYTHING

Did you know that your attitude has an enormous influence over your sales success or failure? In fact, this rises to the level to a natural law, stated as follows by master salesman and speaker, Zig Ziglar:

Law: *Your attitude, not your aptitude, will determine your altitude.*

If you approach a meeting or presentation with nervous apprehension, you set the stage for receiving the same in return. If you make an important phone call while trying to suppress a fear of failure, you create an atmosphere of fear in the conversation.

Too often, salespeople try to cover up internal attitudes of insecurity, worry, and doubt, but end up coming across with a touch of arrogance, superiority, and self-importance. And don't think customers can't tell the difference; because they can.

Even if they don't identify exactly what they're feeling, they sense something that they don't like. And obviously, this is precisely what you're trying to avoid when creating the environment for making a sale, isn't it?

On the other hand, if your attitude is one of confidence, certainty, and positive anticipation, it will change your tone of voice, your body language and the atmosphere around you, making it more comfortable for you and your customer. And isn't this a lot closer to the ideal state for buying decisions to be made?

Okay, if a positive attitude affects your success and you don't have it, how can you get it? The answer is found in these three words:

1. Practice
2. Preparation
3. Confidence

Attitude, for better or worse, is largely build upon confidence. *Confidence* is a reflection of how well you are prepared for the job. And *preparation* is founded in practice.

Now, if it all starts with practice, what's this about?

Practice is when you become so familiar with the tools of your trade that they become second nature. Practice is the time that you work on all your weak spots until they are under your control.

Practice is where you look at all the things that could go wrong, and work out a way to handle each one. Practice is how you align your methods with the basic principles of selling.

Okay, then how does this relate to attitude? Self-disciplined, diligent, focused practice results in being prepared for anything that comes up. When you're prepared, your *confidence is high.*

A high certainty and confidence in doing your job creates a *positive attitude that is infectious.* Concentrated practice and thorough preparation equal an easy confidence and a winning, positive attitude.

Just think this way: *Hard practice equals easy selling.*

It really is just that simple.

ATTENTION FOLLOWS ATTENTION

It may surprise you to know that the most important step in the sales process comes *before you make the first contact.*

What is it? It's what you put your *attention* on.

It is vital that you keep your attention on the *right goal* before you start selling, and that it aligns with your intention.

If all you're worrying about is *"making money,"* or *"making the sale,"* you're setting yourself up for trouble.

Why? Because your attention is on the *wrong purpose.*

When the customer's goal is to get help and your attention is only to get money, don't be surprised when they come up with money worries and concerns out of the blue. Why? Because of this natural law and a self-evident truth.

Law: Attention tends to follow attention.

If your attention is consumed only with sealing the deal, you're ignoring what is important to the client, which is guaranteed to create problems. It's no secret that the customer wants help, service, and a personal benefit from what you're offering. They are not really concerned about the benefit you will get from the sale.

Believe me, the easiest way to be on the same track as your customer, is to have your attention and intention focused on helping customers get what they need and want, then you'll have their agreement. Now you're working together toward a mutually beneficial goal. In this way, you'll have *something in common* with them right off the bat.

It means that you've connected with them on a level that is important to them and that's doing it the easy way. Now, what could be better than that?

Chapter 2

BACK TO BASICS

I've read that if you really want to know your subject, try writing a book. I wholeheartedly agree. It may be humbling, but it provides instantaneous feedback about what you really know or not, by trying to put your thoughts into words.

Personally, what I've discovered is this. If I have any uncertainty about any area of sales - that doubt is exposed when trying to explain it in writing.

Putting thoughts into words on paper so that another can understand easily requires a better understanding than just talking about it.

This is just the tip of the iceberg, but here are four sales maxims (really they are *basic laws*), which express and summarize my feeling about the subject as a reminder:

1. Understand people and you'll understand selling.

2. Mastery of fundamentals is the route toward excellence - not just the accumulation of methods.

3. Knowing why people buy is senior to knowing what they buy.

4. Show the product - sell the dream.

BE WHO YOU REALLY ARE

It's time to tell that whole cast of monsters, demons, bullies and goons to pack up their inane torture devices and go trundling back to the hell from which they crawled.

You haven't got time for the distractions or the negative chatter of small minds mouthing irrelevant, inconsequential opinions.

Living your life waiting for the approval of others is asking their permission for you to live. What a waste of time and your life! Why not *let them worry about what you* think for a change?

Personally, if given a choice, I would *always* rather beg forgiveness than ask for permission.

It takes courage to break the mold of unreal expectations of perfection. It takes courage to ignore the *hidden jury* secretly judging your every action from behind the curtain. It takes courage to face erstwhile opinion leaders formerly looked up to as mentors.

In short, *it takes courage to be who you really are.* But it's still the best thing you can do for yourself. In my opinion, this quote from Ralph Waldo Emerson is perfect.

"To be yourself in a world that is constantly trying to make you something else is the greatest accomplishment."

After all, it's what everyone else wants you to be anyway. It's what distinguishes you from the rest of humanity; it's part of your DNA. It is in your blood. It's you.

The failing is trying to be like everyone else. The courage to disagree, to be different, to stand out from the crowd, to just be you, is an ability. Make it a life-long habit. Don't wait. Start now.

You've got nothing to lose except the self-imposed limitations on yourself. Your life is what you make it.

BUSINESS GOES WHERE IT WANTS

This sales maxim says what it means and means what it says - with universally applicability.

Law: Business goes where it wants - but it stays where it's appreciated.

This principle (understood and applied) will solve most of your problems with retaining existing customers and getting new ones. As one of the biggest expenses is securing new customers, it's far more efficient to keep those you already have, *and keep them happy.*

When businesses lose customers, they typically *assume* it was related to price, a new competitor or even the brother-in-law who now does what you do. Yet research has shown that over 65% of customers leave because of *perceived indifference on the part of the salesperson.*

And as the old adage correctly states: *They don't care how much you know, until they know how much you care. And if you don't care, neither will they!*

Want your job to be more interesting and exciting? This will help:

Law: To become interesting - be interested.

People want to enjoy the sales process as much as they do the product or service. When they really need something, they'll sometimes put up with poor, indifferent service, but not for long!

A sales rep that is more *interested in the customer than they are themselves* will always make the process better for both.

Here is another of my pet peeves; unfortunately, in today's selling environment, *service has become the worst step* in the overall sales process, it's an afterthought at best. What's up with this anyway?

Too often, we find the *sell 'em and forget 'em* attitude among inexperienced sales reps. Service has gotten such a bad reputation that customers routinely *expect to be short-changed* when it comes to getting what they were promised.

I see more people than ever (including myself) driven to wits-end trying to right some wrong as a result of poor service after the sale.

Yes, you can blame the lack of human interaction, outsourcing, careless production standards and shoddy quality control. But personally, I believe that *the nothing matters attitude* is the *source of the problem.*

Too many times, when I complain about sales or service, and say I'm taking my business elsewhere, I'm met with the response from an uncaring clerk, saying or acting like, *who cares?* They simply are unaware (or don't care) that business does have a choice.

Customers don't have to put up with shoddy, careless, unfriendly sales or service, and they never forget how you made them feel (good or bad).

This quote from long-time friend and veteran salesman, Kenny Gordon, applies and also falls into the category of a natural law:

Law: "You have to make a friend to make a sale. Take care of your customers after the sale, and *they'll take care of you.*"

CAN I HELP YOU?

Before we begin, let's get this straight with this natural law of selling.

Law: You're not in the sales business; you're in the people business, focusing on the individual.

You're in the business of helping people get what they need and want. Basically, your job is to contact, connect, and communicate with an individual by providing a product or service that aligns with their purposes and adds value to their lives.

But how often have you heard a sales clerk insincerely mouth the words, "*Can I help you?*" only because some sales trainer told her to do so. I'm sure you're often tempted to ask, "*I don't know, can you?*" I know I am.

It's annoying isn't it?

Some people are touchy about help. Maybe they've been sold on help that was not really helpful, so they feel betrayed, resentful. Now they resist or resent any help from anyone, even it really could help them.

So, if you begin talking about how you can help someone, but your words fall on deaf ears, save your breath; they may be *listening but they're not hearing*. And what's more, their idea of what they *need help with* may be entirely different than yours.

Instead of wasting your time and theirs talking about what you can do for them, why not first *find out if they want help at all*? There is a natural law about this that you must know. You should sell to people who have problems, not those who already have a solution, or *you'll quickly become a problem for the customer:*

Law: Sell solutions to people who have problems.

There are plenty of people who have problems. Once they recognize that they do need help with some problem, the door is open. Ask questions about what they've done to handle the problem in the past. Then ask how it worked out for them, then sell what they want to buy – *not what you need to sell.*

For example, if they say, "We've tried every promotional angle and nothing works." Ask them, "What didn't work?" Let them tell you all the things they've tried before. Most often you'll find that the *program was never done*; it may have been paid for, and started, but left incomplete with no follow up, so *obviously*, the program didn't work.

Another example: They tell you, "We paid for the lead generation program and we didn't get the sales we were promised." Ask them, without threat or challenge, "What was actually done?" Or "Did the leads get into the hands of the salespeople?

And, "Were these people trained to follow up on the lead, get an appointment and a presentation?"

Too many times, you'll find that there was a *weak link in the* selling process, not the lead generation program. But the apparent cause of poor leads quality was only a *red herring*.

As the old proverb states: **"a bad workman always blames his tools,"** when the true source of the problem was *lack of training and apprenticing* within the sales force.

The prospect will want help when he sees that you're addressing the specific issues they're having trouble with. If you can provide help with that, they'll be interested. But this requires that you roll up your sleeves and *get interested* in what's really going on with that prospect. Then you'll be helping the customer where he really needs help, *not just doing what helps you.*

To avoid making trouble for yourself and your prospects, first ask yourself these questions:

1. Do they actually believe they NEED help? If not, find out why not?

2. Do they WANT help? If no, find out why not? Then find the real problem that they need and want help with.

3. Can I actually PROVIDE THE HELP they need and want?

4. WHY is my product or service the best thing for them?

After you've satisfied yourself that you have the correct answers to these questions, you'll discover it's easier to maintain your interest in the customer.

Law: When your focus is entirely on them – their attention will be on you.

CHEAP ADVICE – PRICELESS RESULTS

Listen carefully. This is the cheapest and most valuable advice you'll ever get.

Here it is: *Close the step you're on.*

In fact, the concept is based on this natural law:

Law: *You can't take step two before step one.*

I also discovered very early on in my career that there is more than one close per sale. In fact, there are as many closes as it takes to reach the last one. It's just like walking up stairs.

Question: How many steps are there in a stairway? Answer: As many as it takes to get from point A to point B.

It's the same with selling.

Question: How many steps does it take to close the deal?

Answer: As many as it takes to get from the initial opening to closing the sale.

And if you're smart, you'll take the steps in the selling process *one at a time*. And handle each step thoroughly so that the customer is comfortable on that step before going to the next.

In this way, the final close takes care of itself. It's just *one more step* in the process. The concept is simple.

If you try to shorten the sales process and jump to the closing prematurely, you will meet with resistance and objections. Why? Because you haven't fully completed the prior steps leading to the close. Many people resist change and find it disquieting.

These customers need the earlier steps to gradually and comfortably build up *understanding* before moving into new territory.

Just because you know all about the product or service, doesn't mean they do. You know how others have benefited from what you're offering. But they don't. You know how what you're presenting can benefit them. They don't; at least not yet.

You have to help them climb the stairs, one step at a time.

Your job as a professional salesperson not only requires knowledge of the basic principles of human interaction that underlie all selling, you must also develop methods or techniques that direct and comfortably guide the customer to a result that will benefit both you and the customer. If you fail on either of these two factors (*principles and methods*), you won't even get to first base and a final close is impossible.

Once you realize that *countless small closes* make up the overall process, and the final sales close is just one of many, the stress and effort often associated with the close (for you and the customer) is diminished, if not gone completely.

The next step at any point in the sales process is simply the *close du jour,* the step you should be focusing on that day to move the sale forward.

It's a simple process:

1. Focus on closing the step you're on until it's comfortably complete.

2. Move to the next logical step in the process and close that step.

3. Repeat steps one and two until the final close is done.

Believe me; this way is easier on you and the customer.

BETTER THAN YOU THINK YOU ARE

This concept to follow is as simple as it is powerful, and deserves wider attention.

Once free from the useless baggage of self-denial, unfair comparisons with others and unreasonable demands of perfection in an imperfect world, *you may find that you are better than you think you are.*

We didn't begin life with unreasonable demands of perfection for others or ourselves; nor did we enter into this existence with attitudes of self-criticism or feelings of inadequacy.

Mostly we were just happy to be alive and interact with others who care about us and love us and whom we love and care about. It wasn't all that complicated. We were interested in life and doing the best we could.

But somewhere along the line, *something changed.*

We began to accept the idea that sometimes we didn't win; sometimes things didn't work out as expected, or just like we wanted. And eventually some of us even began to accept the idea that maybe we just weren't up to the challenge. In time, we started settling for *good enough* rather than going for what we really wanted.

But it became even more insidious. Self-doubt began to creep into our consciousness. We developed *bad habits* of wondering and worrying about who we really are, and questioning what we are doing here. Life didn't look as interesting as it once did, but it didn't matter, as now we weren't that interested anyway. Striving to *be the best we can be* didn't seem to be all that it was chalked up to be.

We lost our way and lost sight of who we really were. Instead, we began to believe the lie that we were just not good enough. We reined in our hopes and dreams and accepted "reality" in their place. In short, we let go of our bright-eyed disposition and innate belief in ourselves and in its place, substituted *self-denial* as a habit and a way of life.

But it doesn't have to be that way, if you just accept and let yourself be who you really are, and always have been. Recognizing, acknowledging and accepting the fact that we all have human strengths and weaknesses may be the first step toward allowing you to be you.

No two people are exactly the same and no one person is perfect. In fact, *perfection is a trap* designed to keep you from feeling comfortable in your own skin and be who you really are.

Demanding unreal standards of perfection in an imperfect world only makes the job harder and the emotional toll unnecessarily stressful. While holding to the goal of working toward perfection, isn't it better to accept the fact that it's a never-ending process, not a result in itself.

Life itself could be explained as a work in progress. Maybe a healthy dose of *uncommon sense* should be applied to balance things out. Knowing and accepting who you really are is the first stepping stone to rapid-launch your life again; it reduces stress and makes everything go easier.

It really is not so large a strain to be nice to people; and it enhances their existence and yours at the same time.

If for no other reason, it reduces the stress of normal social intercourse.

Just being interested in and curious about other people tends to make you more interesting and gives their lives a boost at the same time.

Law: Maintaining *an interested attitude* is a key to a happier life.

The unanticipated benefits may include the fact that critical attitudes, jealousies, unreal demands of perfection of self and others tend to fade in importance. Things just don't seem all that serious when you're at ease in your own skin with confidence in yourself.

Unfettered by pretended powerlessness, free from the deadly limitations of self-negation, stripped of the pretentiousness and arrogance that being perfect demands, all that is left is what is really important; *the real you.*

Sooner or later, if you want to get the show on the road, you'll have to admit that *you really are better than you think you are*, and start living with the truth.

Lastly, from the words of Sherlock Holmes in the book "The adventures of Abbey Grange," comes this inspiration:

"Come, Watson, come!" he cried. "The game is afoot."

CHECK YOUR ATTITUDE

"**N**othing can stop the man with the right mental attitude from achieving his goal; nothing on earth can help the man with the wrong mental attitude."

The above quote is from Thomas Jefferson and is one of my favorites.

Every person is clinging to some attitude about life—whether they find it grim, frightening, regretful, maddening or wonderful.

But it's often overlooked that your viewpoint on life is often not governed by reasoning or intellect – rather it is often determined by your *emotions*. Here are some things you should know about this subject:

1. Every emotion comes with a package of fixed responses.
2. The full range of emotions goes from bleak to happy and all stages between.
3. There are subtle layers of restrained emotions, largely unrecognized.
4. Your emotions about yourself can command your attitude about people, things, and life in general and visa versa.

Which leads us to this inevitable conclusion:

Law: Attitudes affect emotions and emotions affect attitudes.

You can't separate these two elements. Also, your attitude can predict your *expectancy* about what will happen in your future – whether positive or negative.

People with a good attitude can envision the future turning out *better than they expected*. And the less willingly a person is to contemplate a desirable future, the lower his chances of winning. This is definitely worth examining. After all, you're the one in charge of creating and choosing your attitudes, aren't you?

Winners consistently expect to win and they exude an attitude with an aura of calm, positive expectancy. Losers seem to expect the reverse. Yes, I know, failure is a part of life, but most of the time, it isn't terminal, as this quote from Winston Churchill states,

Law: "Success is not final, failure is not fatal."

And, it doesn't mean that even if you fail once or a thousand times, that you have to expect that you will always fail. It depends on how you look at it. Thomas Edison had this viewpoint on failure, to which I also subscribe,

"I have not failed. I've just found 10,000 ways that won't work."

Anyone who has reached the top in his or her field knows this simple fact: You don't win every time, but if you *expect to win* every time, you'll tend to win far more than you'll lose.

Sometimes this expectancy alone can *activate your emotions* and give you the determination and persistence to overcome all obstacles.

Legendary basketball star, Isaiah Thomas, agrees:

"I've always believed no matter how many shots I miss, I'm going to make the next one."

Maybe it's time to check your own attitude?

CHRONIC *MAYBE* SYNDROME

Are you spinning your wheels but not gaining traction? Is your life stuck on pause? Can't decide which way to go? Stuck in a state of 6's and 7's (confusion) or indecision, so much so that you just can't get into action on anything?

If all this sounds familiar, you may be suffering from something you've never even heard of.

It's called a Chronic Maybe Syndrome (or C.M.S.). And it means being *stuck in the middle*, indecisive, feeling unable to act or get anything done. It just may be *your worst enemy*, for reasons I will explain. C.M.S. is a trap – because, like a magnet, it attracts *more maybes* to it and creates even more challenges to your initiative, leaving your life chronically *stuck on pause*.

It is a malady characterized by an *inability to make up your mind* – the bane of existence to any salesman or woman – leading to the incapacitating state of being unable to get into action toward any goal, substantially limiting your life activities.

Quite possibly, this factor has ruined more sales careers than any other single element, because it stifles the two most important elements in sales success: *initiative and persistence*.

Now, once you recognize what this disease is about, you'll begin to see that it's not just salespeople that are afflicted with CMS, as many of your *prospects and clients* also exhibit these symptoms.

Gaining an understanding of the cause of this condition will allow you to help your customers *deal with maybes* of their own (a therapeutic action in itself). So, why is it called your worst enemy? Because, *not facing a problem makes it stronger and weakens your resolve to address it.*

The underlying problem starts with the decision that something is too painful to be faced. This is what creates the paralyzing effect of the chronic maybe.

Absent the will to face some obstacle, you instead search for reasons and excuses to avoid it; and you can always find them. But avoiding, fleeing, or pretending a problem doesn't exist does nothing to rectify or cure the situation.

In fact, such actions only camouflage a problem, allowing it to fester and grow worse. Many great thinkers in history agree, and for good reason: For example:

"Facing it, always facing it, that's the way to get through. Face it." – Joseph Conrad.

"All problems become smaller if you don't dodge them, but confront them." - Admiral William (Bull) S. Halsey.

"Most people spend more time and energy going around problems than in trying to solve them." – Henry Ford.

It appears to me that most people believe that looking for a *solution is easier and more interesting than facing a problem directly.* This is because you played a part in creating the problem. Bit by bit, with each tiny compromise of your integrity, each little betrayal of a friend, each small slight of your own abilities, intelligence, and strength, you helped create the problem.

And until you willingly look at the problem, call it what it is, make a decision to do something about it and do it, you are factually *continuing to create it and thus are part of the problem, not the solution.*

The underlying problem, hiding in plain sight, is a confusion or assumption about who the *executive in charge of your life* really is. The bottom line is that *you are the one in charge.* Trying to escape this fact is futile and a waste of time. It is an essential truth that once you *decide your problem is your own*; the best years of your life are yet to be.

The enemy (*chronic maybe syndrome*) is thereby vanquished and your life is once again your own.

Finally, an inspirational quote (really a law in itself) from Roger Crawford, a Hall of Fame athlete while living with a physical challenge affecting all four limbs:

Law: "Being challenged in life is inevitable, being defeated is optional."

CLOSING SALES: THE ESSENTIAL TRUTHS

It's the most coveted, sought-after step in the entire sales process, but nothing produces more worry, anxiety, argument, stress and flop-sweat. What is it? The sales close.

Ultimately *the sales close* is what separates the men from the boys and the neophyte from the master. How you handle this step in the sales cycle can make your career a pleasure or a constant source of tension and distress.

Happily, the basics of closing the sale are not hard to learn and under-stand. Also, it might surprise you to discover that the best closing meth-ods are also the oldest. Why? Because, the natural laws of selling are the underpinning of all the newest and latest methods said to *guarantee* a closed deal. You'll find that *focusing on the principles instead of methods is* the time-honored way to move into the winner's circle consistently.

This article is a primer - focusing primarily on *the essential truths of clos-ing sales*. No matter what you are selling, this approach gives you a solid foundation to strengthen whatever sales closing methods work for you.

So, let's get started.

Short summary

The sales close begins with a friendly contact between you and the customer and finding things you have in common.

This is where *being interested* comes into play.

Next, you build *agreement* on things you have *in common* to gradually strengthen trust and confidence.

Then *clarify their purposes* and find out if their budget aligns with what they want.

Finally, once the prospect sees the personal *benefit* for them, bring the process to a *close*. It really is as simple as that.

But if you've got the wrong tools, or don't know how to use what you do have, you'll be working a lot harder for unsatisfying results. Like trying to cut down a tree with a handsaw, it's frustrating.

The secret to closing sales

The *secret* is that there is that there *is not just one*; there are lots of them. And most of them have already been written in other texts on the subject.

The problem is, the *important secrets are often submerged in an ocean of other useless information.*

Trying to sort through all this to find relatively few bits of truly important and useful data can be maddening. And unless you already know what you're looking for you'll be lost in a sea of confusion.

Closing sales is a *specialized area of the selling process.*

It is when you move from the general idea of generating interest and agreement though selling, to the point where the customer understands the personal benefits that your solution will give them.

They may now be ready to buy, and even want to; *but they still need your help* in getting past the usual barriers that everyone has when parting with their money. Past bad experiences and other things that weren't even there earlier in the process can kick in and thwart the sale. You can handle all of them by correctly using the *tools and techniques of closing*, exhaustively covered in other texts on the subject.

Tactics such as putting their attention back on their on their original purpose for the purchase, summarizing the potential benefits your product or service will provide, reminding them of what problems this would solve for them, what it would feel like to own the new home, car, or computer, etc.

There are as many *methods and techniques of closing* as there are situations, and I advise you to be conversant and comfortable with them.

But focusing only on methods of closing is the *hardest way to get the job done.*

The easiest way to make the closing smooth and effective for both of you is to know and apply the basic principles underlying all methods **before you get to the closing step.**

Okay, here is what I consider to be the *most important secret to closing sales.*

All problems, trouble or stress on closing the sale are caused by one thing; succinctly stated in this law:

Law: All problems in closing stem from an *incomplete or undone step* earlier in the process.

Everything else is a red-herring intended to misdirect, avoid, neglect, justify, rationalize, explain and excuse the fact that you didn't do your job earlier in the process. All the unusual solutions, odd-ball closing methods, desperate moves, forcing the prospect, or worse, getting angry at the customer are a *direct consequence of skipping one of the early steps.*

I can't it say more clearly. It is as simple as it is powerful: if you don't take care of business during the process of selling, closing can be a nightmare.

Do your job from the beginning and the final step is easy.

Recap: Building agreement all the way along is the most important element to closing. The easiest way to do this is by finding common ground between you and the customer and expanding it.

Establishing common ground is, in fact, one of the core skills in contacting, connecting and engaging people. Commonly, your genuine interest in them will always lead you to something you both have in common.

Don't underestimate the power of this simple concept of building agreement. Why? Because, when you try to force someone to agree, you create disagreement and resistance that wasn't there to begin with.

Law: Agreement can't be forced.

Agreement, commonality, or a meeting of the minds, also includes a perceived *personal benefit* in the mind of the customer.

This is the result of carefully planned and executed steps of the overall process leading to this point.

It's what you're looking for, as it signals a very real possibility that the sale will close at this point.

Good question: When is the best time to try to close a sale? Obvious answer: When the customer seems ready to buy.

Most buyers make up their minds to buy only when they understand the personal benefits involved. It doesn't matter what you think or what you say.

If they don't see the benefit for themselves, it doesn't exist. You can't force it or demand it, or become frustrated with them. It's your responsibility to comfortably make it real, in a way that they can accept and understand.

Law: If they say it, it's true. If you say it, it's questionable.

Note: They don't have to tell you their personal reasons about why it's a benefit. You'll see the non-verbal signals anyway so just bring the sale to a close at that point with no further selling.

Remember: Stop selling when the deal is closed. Any selling you do after the sales close is complete will threaten the already closed deal. And, always *stop talking before they stop listening.*

Don't do any selling after the deal is closed. Instead, just go ahead and complete the paperwork as this confirms the sale.

As a salesperson, you're there for one reason: to help the customer. When it looks like they understand the benefits, they may be ready to buy. There is no guarantee, but you should try a trial-close at that point. Good judgment and common sense are in high demand at this point and they are tools you should use liberally. If the trial-close doesn't work, get off it immediately, most likely, you missed a step earlier, or misread their signals.

Sales Personality Types
Question: What *personality type* is the most successful at closing the sale?

Answer: The type that fits best with the customer. The focus should always be on the customer, never on the salesperson.

There are the three primary types:

1. Aggressive
2. Submissive
3. Assertive

You can estimate which group you fall into by evaluating your strengths in these categories:

a) Defining customer needs

b) Establishing and maintaining agreement

c) Controlling the presentation

d) Closing the sale

The overly aggressive type may control every interaction with the customer, but falls short because they believe they know best and fail to gather information on what the prospect really needs and wants. They tend to talk more than they listen.

When the prospect doesn't understand something and resists buying (because of a misunderstanding or disagreement), the aggressive type becomes irritated, forceful, even bullying and overwhelming, which intensifies and creates greater disagreement and sales resistance (the death-knell of any closing possibility).

The submissive salesperson is often excellent with social interaction, over coffee, at dinner in restaurants and other social occasions. They are effective at establishing rapport, but tend to fall down on effectively controlling the sales process.

Too often they simply accept the customers' needs and wants without question (too agreeable). They back off from asking probing questions to further uncover the real problems (too cautious and "nice").

At the close, the submissive salesperson fails to project the comfortable yet effective control necessary to overcome natural trepidation on the part of the customer at parting with their hard-earned cash; and the sale slips away (too timid).

The assertive salesperson is self-confident and self-assured. While controlling the process without forcing the customer, and all the while maintaining open, relaxed communication, they build agreement by genuinely caring about and responding to the customers' needs and wants.

By careful questioning and active listening, they glean valuable information that may not have been otherwise volunteered. By being natural, being yourself and building agreement in comfortable increments, aligning the customers' purposes to what you are selling, and responding to objections with real solutions while maintaining comfortable control, the close becomes somewhat automatic.

It is axiomatic that the salesperson must be *ready to close when the prospect is ready to buy.* It's a mistake to continue selling when it's clear the customer is ready to buy as you can easily talk yourself out of the sale!

Another major reason for failure in closing the sale is that some salespeople never *ask for the order.* Fear that the customer will say "No" has lost many sales. Don't be afraid to ask for the order when the time is right.

Some salespeople use up all their *sales ammunition* too soon and have nothing left. Hold something in reserve if you need it. You'll wish you had, when just one more advantage presented at the right time might have put the sale in the closed column.

There is one primary purpose for studying sales principles and natural laws of selling: *To help the prospect get what they need and want.*

The fact that you experience a personal benefit from increased confidence in your skills is *secondary* to the primary purpose of your job.

Always keep in mind that all you're ever doing is trying to help the customer find a solution to their problems, not yours.

Sales pressure vs. force
This subject must be looked at although some may find it uncomfortable to do so. Just remember these two facts:

Sales pressure is your friend. Force is your enemy.

Many salespeople shy away from using sales pressure, often because they don't understand it or they confuse it with force. This is a mistake. Don't be afraid of using pressure when called for in closing the sale.

The dictionary states that pressure is something that affects thoughts and behavior in a powerful way. This is not a negative thing.

Sales pressure is another way of saying you care about the customer and you're convinced that what you're offering is the best solution for their problems.

Customers generally do not mind sales pressure when appropriate, but they uniformly hate being forced to buy. Learn to tell the difference.

People have different tolerances of how much pressure is acceptable and when it seems like they are being forced.

Just remember: Pressure is welcome if it helps the customer make tough decisions. Force is always resisted and always resented. Don't do it.

Objections

Some salespeople avoid objections. My guess is that they fail to recognize that "No" doesn't always mean "No." Mostly, it means you haven't done your job on the earlier steps. In any case, you should not shrink from handling this important step.

Remember if you never ask for the order, you'll never hear "No," but, you'll also never hear "Yes."

Example: Let's assume you have already qualified the customer and they can afford what you're selling. Also, you have established that they need and want what you're offering. Now, the final step is to seal the deal.

Question: How do you do this?

Answer: Ask for the offer, "Cash or check?" or "Let's get started, shall we?"

If they say, "Yes," you say, "Good," then start the paperwork immediately.

If they say, "No," then you handle as necessary in the simplest way possible that still gets the result.

Example: They start to doubt their decision to move ahead with the deal:

You say, "Well, you do want (product or service) don't you"? Then, "Let's get it done today."

If they come up with a general objections that can't be handled right then, you say, "That's an interesting point of view. Let's take a look at that."

Then you get it down to specifics so they come off the generality. Get them gradually off the generalized stop or slow and remind them of what they really want. Then show them how they can get what they wanted.

Example: If they say, "I'm going to do it, but I've got to work out the money. I'll get back to you after I go home and figure it out." You say, "Well, what exactly do you have to figure out"?

They'll squirm around a bit because the excuse they have given is not the truth. Get them through it and you'll help them get what they really want.

Note: there should be no objection from them at you offering to help, if that is really the issue. If it isn't, then find the right problem.

As the salesperson, you have to be able to face the back off and barriers that you may have on asking people for money. You cannot shrink from those barriers. You cannot be timid or careful about asking people about these areas and helping the prospect get past the mental barriers that are stopping them (likely in more ways than one).

Your job is to help the customer and *add value* to their lives. The closing step is where you help them move past the obstacles stopping them from getting what they really need and want.

Help the customer by being on their side. If you're not, you become the problem.

Keep their attention on the result not the process and you'll close more deals with less effort. To turn mystery into mastery in closing the sale, remember these points:

Natural Selling

Closing the sale starts with the first contact with the customer.

The sales close is just the last step in the overall selling process, no more or less important than any other.

Building agreement (common ground) throughout the sales process takes the stress out of buying.

Here are a few natural maxims (natural laws) of selling I've come across that deserve your attention:

> *Uncertainty, doubt and fear* caused by *stress* are primary barriers to closing a sale.

> People don't buy products or services; they buy potential *solutions* to their problems.

> Sell what they want to buy, not what you need to sell.

> Keep your attention on *adding value* to the customer, not on the money.

> Maintaining comfortable control during the selling process eliminates the need for force.

> The main cause of difficulty with closing the sale is an *incomplete handling* of the earlier steps.

> Don't be afraid *to ask for the order* when the time is right.

People generally like buying. They dislike being sold, and they *hate being forced.*

Yes, usually comes as one word, but *No,* is commonly accompanied with reasons why not.

Magical closing methods or *miraculous* techniques will not work if the prospect is not prepared for buying.

Force is your greatest enemy of closing, as it creates resistance and disagreement. Pressure is not force.

Sales pressure means caring about the customer combined with the conviction that your solution is the best for them.

Agreement = the possibility of a closed sale. Disagreement = guaranteed no sale.

Natural laws and basic principles are few. Methods are infinite. Principles drive methods, not the reverse.

Help the customer get what they want and they'll give you what you need.

COMMUNICATION: Magic or Tragic?

This may be the most important article I've written on selling because it explores both the most common *reasons for success and the primary reasons for failure.*

It's about *communication,* a word that is abused and misused so often it's amazing we get along at all.

Simply stated: To any aspiring or veteran salesperson, *communication is the key to success* at all levels of selling.

Excellence as a salesman or woman simply cannot be attained without becoming a skilled communicator. Yes, it really is that important, but sadly, the art and skill of communication is rarely given the importance it deserves, even at universities that should know better.

Even when it is touched on, they focus mainly on sophomoric techniques and methods of public speaking, never dealing with the vital fundamental elements of the subject. Yet success in life is intimately related to your ability to communicate and build relationships.

The obvious truth is that communication is as much about the *messenger* as it is the *message*.

Law: In selling, you are the **messenger and the message.**

And what you're saying may be less important than *how you say it*. Everything about you as the messenger; the way you dress, your tone of voice, body language, how you move or gesture, what words you emphasize, the volume, your pace, words, acknowledgements or lack of them, enunciation, which words you accent, what words you repeat, are all signals that convey a message.

Are you being professorial, demanding, lecturing, too stiff, unapproachable, distant, assertive, pushy or forceful in trying to get someone to listen to you or agree with you? Even appearing too fearful, weak, unconfident or uncertain can sabotage your message.

What are you trying to achieve with your communication? Impress them with how learned and erudite you are (the messenger)? Or express your message in a manner that will ensure it is received exactly as intended?

Everything you say or do - or don't say or do – is either doing useful work for you or it's working against you.

Understand: When I use the word communication, I'm not talking about the superficial ability to read a prompter, a power-point slide, or a prepared, memorized script. The essence of true communication is found in a deep, visceral, gut-level understanding of the inner workings of the subject and the importance of reaching the people you're talking to and building a relationship.

In any case, whether inborn or learned, gaining the ability to talk easily and convincingly (sometimes called "the gift of gab") with people can catapult you to success in selling.

No matter how large or small the audience, the skill of connecting and making each individual feel you are speaking to them personally, touching their emotions and conveying the message that what you're talking about has something to do with their lives puts you in the driver's seat.

Such skills also include the effortless ability to think and speak at the same time, being able to listen and hear what they are not saying, and to shift gears seamlessly when necessary.

The ability to smoothly discover what they need and want must be thoroughly mastered so that it is instinctive and as natural as falling rain.

Master communicators are not only great listeners, but also excellent observers of the micro indicators that we all give off that expose our thoughts and feelings, intentionally or not.

What appears magical or superhuman to others is just a normal day on the job to the great communicators; as such abilities are the core competencies for entrance to the winner's circle. So, let's take a look behind the curtain and how this thing really works, shall we?

One-Minute Summary:
Communication is the activity of conveying or receiving thoughts, ideas, feelings, and information; derived from the Latin word "communis" - meaning "common" or "to share."

Your communication skills are the methods you use to apply this concept. As in selling, it's all about finding commonality with others.

For example: people like people who like them, and who are like them. The more you have in common, the more agreement and greater potential for effective communication.

People often feel that because they can talk, that they are communicating; and in social situations this is generally accepted as true.

But in the business of selling, the stakes are higher. A professional salesperson must *communicate with a purpose*. Small talk with no purpose doesn't cut it.

This quote, with which I agree is from my friend Randy Vadar; it states this concept perfectly:

"The greatest prerequisite for a communicator is not the technique with which they communicate - it is having something to say!"

"Having something to say," means that you are *communicating with a purpose*. Initially your purpose should be to find out what you have in common with the customer.

For example, if you both have the purpose of finding the right product or service at the right price, most difficulties melt away when you're both working toward the same goal with the same purpose.

Now, the anatomy of any problem can be traced back to opposing purposes, and as you don't want to become a problem for a prospective client, your goal should be to master both *verbal and nonverbal communication skills.*

Most people find face-to-face communication uncomfortable, especially when confrontational. They would prefer to avoid such things at all cost. But very often, face-to-face communication, nonverbal communications such as body language and physical impressions can have more impact than spoken words if done correctly. Even written communications can further your purposes or stop them cold by conveying the wrong message when done incorrectly.

The process of communicating requires skill in correctly observing, speaking, listening, questioning, evaluating and responding appropriately. Any weakness or breakdown in any one of these factors will have *negative effects*.

What salespeople must understand is that communication is both the taking in of another's ideas (inflow) and the relaying of one's own ideas (outflow). If a prospect has inhibitions on the outflow of communication, it's like pulling teeth to find out what is really troubling them. If they have difficulty on inflow, you may be talking but they're not taking it in.

From the salesperson's side, inhibitions in outflowing communication can end up with never asking for the order and other weaknesses. Hang-ups on the inflow mean not listening to what the customer is saying leading to miscommunications and assumptions – never a good idea. Misuse or mishandle either inflow or outflow of communication between you and the customer and *tragic results* are pretty much guaranteed. But, using purposeful communication skills with finesse can create *magical* results.

The Inside Scoop
First, you must realize that you're not in the sales business - you're in the people business, *helping the individual.* This one small change in your focus (*from people in general to the individual specifically*) in selling can often create enormous changes in your success ratio.

After all, you're not in the business of selling to people or talking to people, you're in the business of *communicating with an individual.*

There must be an interchange of some kind for live communication to occur. Canned, scripted, rote recitation of your sales pitch is just about as effective as talking to a wall.

There must be an exchange of information and interchange of ideas or communication doesn't exist, by definition.

It should be better known that most communication failures can be traced to *false, or uninspected assumptions or preconceptions.* For example: When you *assume* someone understands what you're saying, you're making a big leap of faith, very often unfounded.

Assuming that you know best about what someone wants, and to then begin talking about that subject, you may be way off the mark and not even know it. Don't be surprised when they stop listening.

Communication is the *stock in trade* (the core competence) of any salesperson, so let's not fall into the same trap of *assuming* we know all about this subject; certainly we can all improve on our skills, no matter how experienced. So, to establish a starting point in understanding what we're talking about, here is what the dictionary says about the subject.

Communication is defined as, "the act of transmitting or exchanging information, making something known; to connect one with another."

In layman's terms, it just means trying to get your ideas across to someone else by finding what you have in common. In either case, the concept has to do with establishing a *connection* to facilitate an *interchange*.

Note: *connection and interchange* are the operative words.

Whatever else occurs, if a connection and interchange of ideas didn't take place, you can rule out any communication - or a sale - taking place. When you establish a connection and create a smooth interchange, then we can say that communication has been established. This is what opens the door to the *possibility* of making a sale. But if your communication is never received by anyone it becomes a solitary exercise in mis-communication or no-communication.

Now, theoretically there might be some therapeutic value in this much like punching a heavy bag for thirty or forty minutes, but for our purposes it is useless.

Without getting overly philosophical about it, there simply has to be someone putting something out there and connecting with someone else, leading to a willing interchange of ideas.

Operating Definition.

Minimally then, as an *operating definition*, we can say that communication is composed of at least the following two factors:

A. The *exchange* of the ideas we deliver, (the sales presentation and other information), and the ideas the prospect delivers, (regarding their concerns, etc.).

B. The *connection,* which strengthens the agreement and mutual interest of both parties. If they don't understand it or if it's not helpful or useful to them, then it's just raw, unevaluated data; no real connection is established and the communication does not have any value. Communication of data alone may be rejected as suspect or unimportant when one person alone says it.

As you get them more and more involved, the purposes of both the salesman and the prospect become undeniably aligned and you can almost feel it *sizzle.*

It becomes laser-like in its focus, will cut through anything in its way, and is almost impossible to stop. This is where the communication skills of the professional salesman can make or break the day. When the prospect feels he *understands the benefits* and begins to assume ownership of the product or service, the salesman must recognize the *possibility for a close* (the trial close) and skillfully bring it to a happy conclusion.

The longer you screw around after the point when the customer has seen a true benefit for themselves, the more likely it is that something else will come up to be handled. So, just wrap it up as smoothly as possible and put their attention down the road on the next step in the overall process.

Mutual Interest.

Establishing commonality will serve the interests of all concerned by getting everyone on the same page at the same time, gaining agreement, and creating *co-motion* (mutual motion in the same direction at the same time).

Besides finding things you have in common, the most effective way to get someone interested in you is to be interested in them. This is counter-intuitive, but remarkably effective.

Interest is curiosity.

When you are interested in anything, it tends to create a mental or physical *reach or desire* in the direction of whatever has attracted your attention. If you can find something interesting about people, they will become more interested in you. This falls back on a well-known maxim: *attention follows attention*. When your attention is on them, their attention will usually be on you.

It naturally follows that if you approach the prospect with your attention completely on finding *a way you can help them*, their attention will usually follow suit.

If your attention is only on the commission you will earn from the sale, their attention will go onto money as well. They will unconsciously bring up money as an issue and often thwart the sale.

In spite of a cavalier attitude from the prospect – looking unbothered and showing little or no concern for important or serious problems, saying, for example, "it's not really a problem, everything is under control"– extensive experience has conclusively proved one thing: No matter what they're saying to the contrary, there are always family issues, business problems, and other worries, stresses or hidden cold-sweat issues grabbing their attention, to a greater or lesser degree, hiding just below the surface. And *that is precisely where your interest and attention* must be if your purpose is to help them where they need it.

The enemy here is the overly talkative salesman, who apparently feels they are so "*interesting*" that any effort to be "*interested*" is moot. Instead, to succeed, you have to foster a fertile relationship of *two-way communication* by adjusting the talking and listening ratio as indicated. This is how successful sales are conceived, nurtured, grown, and finally delivered. Happily, there is a secret weapon you use to create that environment.

The secret revealed.
One mistake many beginning salesmen and women (and even veteran salespeople) make is this: they try to *solve their own problems first and the customer's problems second.*

This can cause trouble because it is not in agreement with this natural law:

Law: Customers are always interested in their own problems more than they are in yours.

The first thing to do, in any normal sales procedure, is to introduce yourself and your product or service in quick, broad strokes, then ask a question; ask about something you are *sincerely interested* in knowing; something you're really curious about. You want to find out what's bugging them, what's worrying them, what's got their attention that they feel they can't do anything about.

You don't have to sweat at this too hard; just ask the right questions (with sincere interest), then listen, and you won't be able to shut them up.

Believe me, they're looking for help in some area of their life, and if you're the right person to talk to, *they will tell you all about it.*

Do this using your five best selling friends: *why, how, when, who, and where.* Almost any variety of questions will work - if you just use them.

Three important things happen when you do this.

1. You withdraw slightly; thus creating some space that will allow him to reach toward you and contribute something of his own.
2. You find out more about him through his answers.
3. You remain in the drivers' seat.

Law: Communication is a reciprocal process of reaching and withdrawing by both parties.

When you ask a question you are *reaching*, while shutting up for a second or two or asking a question is a form of *withdrawing* - inviting something from the other person allowing them to contribute if they wish.

As a sales professional, you have to let the prospect in on the process. Let them add something; let them ask a question if they want; let them fill up the space verbally or mentally. Thus, the chain of events would be to reach toward the prospect with a question, then withdraw and listen to what they say in response and respond accordingly.

If you relax and give them a chance, they will often not only tell you *what they want,* but also *what you need to know* to solve their problem.

My brother Chuck Jacobs uses this concept to good advantage in his business when defusing a tense situation, by simply saying,

"Now, help me out here - - - " then asking the prospect a question designed to get them talking to help clarify any generalized objections. Then listen carefully to the responses to these questions to *ferret out the real objection,* as often the first objection is not the real one.

Next, let them contribute, and solicit their help in handling any difficulties discovered. Sometimes simply asking honestly, "What would you like me to do about that?" will work wonders in resolving stuck points.

Next is the step that deserves the most attention, but often ends up with the least.

Listen:
These two quotes speak volumes, simply and clearly:

"Most of the successful people I've known are the ones who do more listening than talking." —Bernard M. Baruch

"There's a lot of difference between listening and hearing." - G.K. Chesterton.

While communications skills have two main components of equal importance: speaking and listening, you would be remiss not to include hearing what is really being said (or not being said). This is where top producers shine. It's not what you say - but how well *you hear what the other person is saying* that's important.

Listening means "to give one's attention to; to take note" and is at once the most obvious and neglected tool in any selling activity.

It is also why this law holds true:

Law: Your ears are often your best selling tools.

Interested, attentive listening will dig you out of more sticky situations than you can imagine, as most people are desperate for someone to really listen to them. It shouldn't need to be said that once you've come this far, if you're doing all the talking, you will only discover *what you already know.* You'll never discover any of the difficulties, problems, concerns, or objections of the prospect if they are not given a chance to talk. So, when you ask that question, sit back, inhale nice and slow and *really actively listen* to what your prospect is telling you.

Then, when it's your turn to talk again, address what the prospect has told you as completely as necessary.

Note: this step can be overdone; if they only want to know what time it is, don't explain how to build a watch. Give them what they need, not more, not less. Align your answer to what information he or she needs to feel comfortable, not to how much you may know about the subject.

As an additional note, listening should not be confined only to the times when the prospect is talking. You must also be listening and observing while speaking. The prospect communicates through their body language, facial expression, eye contact or lack thereof, and many other subtle ways.

They are trying to tell you something, and unless you are *listening with your eyes* - and other sense perceptions - you will miss vital information.

The punch line:

The big punch line here is that the whole enterprise becomes easy if you simply break it down to its basic concepts:

You establish active, live (not canned) communication by whatever effective means at your disposal, being genuinely interested in the prospect, remaining curious about their goals and purposes, and determining how you can help them.

You impart useful information, (not just data), that they can understand and use by any communication channel available, and orient your product or service to their *needs and wants*.

You communicate further, simultaneously listening to their opinions and ideas, while building *agreement, confidence and trust* based on mutual interest and understanding. You demonstrate how their interests will be served and how this represents a personal *benefit to them* directly. Until this light bulb of understanding goes on and they see why it is to their *advantage* to do business with you, you can't consider that they are "sold."

Keep it simple - strive to simplify.
Insecurity creates complexity. And complexity creates insecurity. Direct, open communication is best. Precise, clear communication comes from *confidence* in your product and service, and *certainty* that you can deliver what you promise. Keep it clear, direct, simple, and human; you'll both win.

Jack Welch, Chairman of General Electric, said it this way:

"You can't believe how hard it is for people to be simple, how much they fear being simple. They worry that if they're simple, people will think they're simple-minded. In reality, of course, it's just the reverse. Clear, tough-minded people are the most simple."

There is nothing to fear from being straightforward and uncomplicated in your communication. By doing so, you will have eliminated the most common reasons for failure – being convoluted and confusing.

The prospect is probably telling you over and over in subtle ways exactly what they want from you and your company. Show them how they can get what they want - *they'll help you close the deal.*

Think about that for a second, customers are telling you how they can be sold, but you'll never know unless you're really paying attention to what they're saying.

Do the usual.
When you neglect the natural laws of communication, you resort to inventing unusual solutions or untried methods to get someone to do business with you. This adds complexity to the process and moves you farther away from a simple A to B approach. It is the wise man that can reduce the activity to the fundamental principles and find workable methods, and then apply both of them consistently and flawlessly.

Of course, that is all we expect of you as a professional in sales. Align your methods to basic principles; practice methods that align with the basics, and get used to seeing *magical results* as the norm instead of the exception.

Chapter 3

COURAGE

Let's tell it like it is: selling requires courage. Rejection and rebuff go with the territory and taking such things personally can terminally stunt your career potential.

So what is this thing called courage anyway? One thing for sure, it's linked to the *emotion of fear* in no small degree, even though it is *basically an attitude* that can help or hinder your career.

This quote from Henry Ford illustrates: "Whether you think you can, or you think you can't – you're right."

Courage is made up of certain native or acquired mental qualities like bravery, boldness, audacity, and a willingness to face things head on without flinching.

In fact, the first step to *handling* anything is the idea that you can face it. It is a *practiced ability* that allows you to face and move past your fears instead of trying to avoid them. Also it is not static; rather it grows stronger with practice and weakens from disuse.

You may not have noticed that you can shrink back from confronting something, *and then feel fear*. It is not necessarily true that you must feel the fear first.

It could be that your experiences in life have trained you to believe something is fearful, or embrace fear as a *reason or excuse* to explain why you didn't face up to something in the first place. Also, the emotion of fear can sometimes kick in *after you decide* something is *too painful to experience*.

Law: Courage is not the absence of fear - it's being willing to continue in spite of your fear.

Fear is after all, just a *natural emotion* like many others. It is rarely fatal. In fact it can come in very handy at the right time. But if overdone, it tends to diminish your ability to face and conquer the ordinary obstacles and challenges of life.

As Ralph Waldo Emerson says, "Fear defeats more people than any other one thing in the world."

Courage is the reverse; it is a *chosen attitude* that can lead to growth and expansion. It also allows you to increase the size of the challenges you are willing to face without flinching, opening the door to increased happiness, success and expansion.

Many great thinkers agree:

John Kenneth Galbraith, "All of the great leaders have had one characteristic in common, it was the *willingness to confront.*"

Eleanor Roosevelt, *"You gain strength, courage, and confidence by every experience in which you really stop to look fear in the face. You are able to say to yourself, 'I lived through this horror. I can take the next thing that comes along.'"*

Dale Carnegie, "You can conquer almost any fear if you will only make up your mind to do so. For remember, fear doesn't exist anywhere except in the mind."

Marianne Williamson, "Our deepest fear is not that we are inadequate. Our deepest fear is that we are powerful beyond measure."

Georgia O'Keeffe, "I have been absolutely terrified my entire life, and I have *never let it keep me from doing* a single thing that I wanted to do."

Sir Winston Churchill, "Courage is rightly esteemed the first of human qualities because it is the quality, which guarantees all others."

Law: Courage trumps fear every time.

My humble opinion is simply this: the essence of courage is *doing what you've got to do when you've got to do it* - in spite of all the reasons, excuses, and justifications to do otherwise.

Only those things that you believe you cannot face can control you. Face your fears and they no longer control you; they fade instead into insignificance - like the shadows that they really are.

Law: Your attitude in the present can change your future, just as your attitude about the future can change your present.

Circumstances don't dictate your attitude; *your attitude creates your circumstances*. The choice is ultimately your own.

CREATE YOUR OWN LUCK

You can't buy it and you can't sell it . . .

And what's more, the harder you try to hold on to it, the more likely it is to vanish faster than a gambler's lucky streak.

Because, whether good luck or misfortune, it is not a thing; most often, it's the *label* we put on something that has already happened. So, assuming that we all would prefer good luck to the opposite, what is this thing called luck? The following might give us some insight. It is from a real-life story about creating your own luck, by seeing opportunity in problems, and by expanding into the demand.

As the story goes, if you were in the market for a pocket watch in 1880, where would you get one? If you wanted the best watch, you went to the train station. This is because the station agents were also skilled telegraph operators, which was the primary method of communication with the railroad stations in those days. Of course, they had to know precisely when trains left the previous station and when they were due at their next station, so the telegraph operators *had to have the best watches.*

A man named Richard, a telegraph operator himself, was one who could see opportunity where others only saw a problem. He was on duty in the North Redwood, Minnesota train station one day when a load of watches arrived from the East. It was a huge crate of pocket watches but no one ever came to claim them. So Richard sent a telegram to the manufacturer and asked them what they wanted to do with the watches. The manufacturer didn't want to pay the freight back, so they wired Richard to see if he could sell them.

And sell them he did, by sending a wire to every agent in the system asking them if they wanted a cheap, but good, pocket watch. He sold the entire case in less than two days and at a handsome profit.

Then things started getting interesting. He ordered more watches from the watch company and encouraged the telegraph operators to set up a display case in the station offering high quality watches for a cheap price to all the travelers. It didn't take long for the word to spread and, before long people other than travelers *came to the train station to buy watches.*

Richard became so busy that he had to hire a man named Alvah, a professional watchmaker, to help him with the orders. The business took off and soon expanded to many other lines of dry goods. Richard and Alvah left the train station and moved their company to Chicago -- and it's still there.

The name of the company started by Richard Sears and his partner Alvah Roebuck was *Sears, Roebuck and Co.* From its mail order beginnings, the company grew to become the largest retailer in the United States by the mid-20th century, and its catalogs became world-famous.

Where others saw only problems, he saw opportunity and went into action to expand into the demand.

Brian Tracy hits the mark on this point:

"I've found that luck is quite predictable. If you want more luck, take more chances. Be more active. Show up more often."

You'll find opportunities all around you. But most will walk right by them without the slightest glance; all the while keeping their attention focused on reasons to explain why they aren't lucky.

Finally, I want to pass a surprisingly effective tip for attracting good luck:

Good luck can't find you if nobody's home. It may be looking for you but will never find you if you're not being yourself.

As Mr. Tracy says, "take more chances, be more active, and **show up more often**."

CREDIBILITY IN SELLING

Everyone agrees that credibility is a valuable commodity. But in selling, it is *indispensable.*

You either have it, get it, or you won't make the grade in sales. You can't force anyone to think you are credible. It's invisible, intangible, and seemingly unattainable if you're not born with it, but obvious to everyone when you have it.

Credibility is something that permeates your entire being. It's perceptible yet untouchable, abstract but obvious, *visible and invisible* at the same time. As is said of some of the more salacious elements in society, *"you know it when you see it."*

Okay, if it's so important, where can I get some of this stuff?

The key to credibility is *trustworthiness*, and this is made up of a combination of personal integrity, honesty and your reputation.

If you fail to get people to *trust you*, you might as well pack it up. Nothing will go well without it. Steven Covey says it this way:

"Trust is the glue of life. It's the most essential ingredient in effective communication. It's the foundational principle that holds all relationships."

Some claim that the only way to make a man trustworthy is to trust him. I agree, to an extent, as to think that trustworthiness is determined only *externally* is a bit narrow, at least to me.

I believe that before others see you as worthy of trust, you have to trust yourself first. And the easiest way of trusting yourself is to *be honest with yourself.*

We've all got this handy-dandy, internal monitor constantly watching what we say and listening to what we do, and keeping score. Honesty starts at home every day when you look in the mirror. Honesty equates to being trustworthy. And it starts with you.

What's more, customers are not stupid. They can sense when they're getting a sales pitch and you're not being straightforward.

Yes, you can become quite facile at convincing yourself and others of your honesty and trustworthiness. But words are cheap and trust is dear.

You are not instantly honest or worthy of trust only because you say so. You can't force anyone to believe you are credible. Establishing the bond of trust with the customer takes as long as it takes, and it's based on actions.

Sometimes they want to test you out and see if you actually do *deliver what you promise.*

They'll give you a small order and see how you do. If you're on time and provide what you promised, confidence and trust will increase and credibility builds. It is then easier to leverage this into a bigger order next time.

Once you do hold the position in their mind as being *reliable, credible and trustworthy*, guard it as you would any other valuable thing, as it is much easier to gain the position in the first place than to regain it once lost.

Recap: There is only one reliable way to get others to like you and trust you: *You must like and trust yourself first.*

And the only way to really trust and like you, is to first *be honest with yourself*. When you do, you become credible to yourself. Then you'll find that people magically also see you as *trustworthy and credible*. It's the easiest and most effective way to get the job done.

DEBUGGING THE CLOSE

The term "debugging" is popularly attributed to U.S. Navy Rear Admiral Grace Hopper. While she was working on a Mark II computer at Harvard University, a moth was discovered stuck in a relay, which impeded the operation. As the story goes, she said that they were *debugging* the system; thus the word was coined.

I've often used the word when *debugging* a delicate sales closing situation with sales people and I always begin with this statement: *"Don't tell me about the sale, tell me about the people."*

Why? Because long, hard-won experience has taught me one simple fact: adjusting your closing techniques or methods will not solve the problem - **look to the basic principles first.**

That's where you'll find both the problems and the solutions to all bugged sales closings. You will always have trouble unless you learn and use this basic principle:

Law: Handle the people first and business will take care of itself.

So, consider yourself forewarned, if you try to skip this step or rush through it quickly just to seal the deal – it will come back to bite you! So, my advice: don't make *trouble* for yourself. Spend as much time as needed to fully handle the people; this will always make the business side of things go much, much smoother.

They'll feel better about the purchase and you'll feel better about the sale. Because at the end of the day, it's always about the people anyway, isn't it?

ELIMINATING CLOSING ANXIETY

Okay, everyone knows that *closing sales* means pay and increased survival, right? But why is there is so much *anxiety* connected with this particular step? After all, it's just one more step on the ladder isn't it?

Maybe a look at the inner workings and causes of anxiety might provide a better understanding.

At lower levels, anxiety is just a slight, uneasy feeling of concern, worry, or dread, sort of a low-level fear. You commonly feel this as a normal reaction to facing something for which you are *not prepared*.

Taken to extremes it can be intimidating and overwhelming, creating a feeling of being paralyzed, unable to function; your attention is fixed on "*what if…*" negative scenarios of failure instead of feelings associated with winning.

The lower levels of anxiety we can usually handle, but the higher levels can often present a bigger challenge.

As the common denominator of anxiety and stress is a *real or imagined threat to survival*, it's obvious that no sales closings equals no income, which equates to a threat to survival. This alone can create anxiety and stress. But there are other less obvious factors at work.

Things like your own purpose of being successful at your chosen profession, your future goals, your family obligations, self-confidence, morale, group standing and reputation all come into play and are affected by how well you do your job. But the key to controlling and even eliminating sales anxiety is building up your self-confidence, meaning you are certain of your abilities and your judgment.

It is the self-assured feeling of trust in yourself that you can do the job you have been trained to do and get good results.

It is the freedom from doubt about whether you can do what is called for. Anxiety and doubt *do not coexist* with confidence. Okay then, if confidence is so important, where can we get some? This, too, is pretty simple.

Confidence grows with practice. And practice is composed of exposure to the area you are learning and disciplined, correct repetition. Then, correct repetition of the fundamentals of the discipline will lead to confidence and absence of anxiety.

It's said that some practice until they can get it right; this is commendable and a worthy goal of an amateur. But others continue to practice and practice even more, until they eliminate chances of getting it wrong. This is where top professionals live.

Practice builds the self-assurance and confidence that you can do something to professional standards every time.

This is what creates the internal security that you can handle whatever comes up and get a favorable outcome.

Practice trains the muscle memory that eventually becomes second nature, so failure is not even an option.

Then even under stressful conditions, you don't have to think or remember what to do. You just do it effortlessly.

How long does this take? Bluntly, it takes as long as it takes. It's different for each individual. But three things are certain:

1. Anxiety is conquered by building confidence.
2. Confidence is increased through focused preparation and disciplined practice.
3. Practice is based on exposure and correct repetition.

These quotes by people at the top in their fields support this concept:

"Confidence doesn't come out of nowhere. It's a result of something... hours and days and weeks and years of constant work and dedication." - Roger Staubach

"One important key to success is self-confidence. An important key to self-confidence is **preparation**." - Arthur Ashe

"Winning breeds confidence and confidence breeds winning." - Hubert Green

"If you want to be good, you have to practice, practice, practice. If you don't love something, then don't do it." - Ray Bradbury

"Confidence awakens confidence." - Friedrich Von Sachsen

Don't practice until you get it right. Practice until you can't get it wrong. – *Unknown*

"Confidence is contagious. So is lack of confidence." - Michael O'Brien

And one of my personal favorites:

"Own the room. Confidence has nothing to do with what you look like. If you obsess over that, you'll end up being disappointed in yourself all the time. Instead, high self-esteem comes from how you feel in any moment. So walk into a room acting like you're in charge, and spend your energy on making the people around you happy. Giving confidence to others

will come back to you and you'll end up feeling better about yourself." — Marian Seldes, celebrated American actress.

Confidence and anxiety alike thrive on and are nourished by the attention you give them. Which one shows up depends on you and which one you cultivate.

Law: Confidence is not a condition, it's a result.

EMOTION: THE SECRET WEAPON

Okay, I admit it.

I had fallen into the same trap I'd advised others not to do - a potentially dangerous oversight. I assumed everyone knew what I was talking about when I said that *emotion was the bridge to action.*

Myrna Jacobs, my wife - at once my strongest advocate and outspoken critic - gave me the whack on the side of the head I needed when she asked, "*Why do you say that emotion is the secret to every sale?*" I replied, "*Err, umm, ah, well, you know – it's how you feel, everyone knows that don't they?*"

While fumbling around trying to maintain an erudite, learned façade, I managed to retrieve my trusty, dog-eared dictionary.

I quickly discovered this: emotion is a mental state that arises spontaneously; a feeling. But it was the derivation of the word that really drove the point home. The word, emotion comes from Old French esmovoir, *to excite,* and from Latin movere, *to move.*

Wait just a minute! Did I read that right? Did it really say, ***to excite and to move?***

Yes, it certainly did – and *to move and to excite* is the goal of any salesperson, isn't it? Suddenly it all fell into place. I knew I had discovered the *key that unlocked the lock:* Emotion is the key to all selling.

Why? Because this is what gets people *excited* and makes them *move into action.*

And how do you get a prospect to move from thinking about it, to doing something? The answer is as simple as it is profound: touch them emotionally. If you don't get them emotionally involved, you're just talking.

Now this was getting *exciting!*

I was looking at this for a moment longer when suddenly the penny dropped. I realized this:

When customers see a *personal benefit* for themselves, they simultaneously get an *emotional reaction* and feel like going into *action.*

They get *excited - and they want to move* (exactly as it says in the derivation of the word *emotion*)

You've reached them emotionally when they can relate to what you're saying, and can *imagine a personal benefit from* doing business with you. This is what gets them excited so they feel like going into motion.

Emotion really is the secret weapon, the magnet that attracts and draws the prospect into wanting to do something. It takes the prospect out of the realm of logic or thinking about it and puts them into motion.

Law: Logic makes people think. Emotion makes people act.

The entrance point to *emotion* is to discover what the individual prospect considers a personal *benefit.* If they feel it, they'll believe it; and if they believe it, they will find a way to buy it. On reflection, the combination of these two factors may well be the *single most important discovery* I've ever made in researching the area of sales and selling.

Law: *Emotion* is the human element, the bridge that touches the imagination and causes people *to feel excited* and *want to move into action.*

And that occurs when they perceive or imagine a *personal benefit* for themselves in what you're offering.

It's said that all basic truths are as simple as they are powerful. This one does not disappoint.

EXPAND OR CONTRACT?

You either expand or you contract, and if you're not expanding . . . you're contracting.

Law: Change is the only constant.

It's been said there are no absolutes in this universe, but the fact of the *inevitability of change* comes pretty close. You're either going up or you're going down, you can never stay level forever. As my aunt Virginia Miller used to say to me: "Things will change."

Great thinkers agree:

"The only constant in life is change." – Heraclitus, a Greek professor.

And from Stephen Covey:

"There are three constants in life . . . change, choice and principles."

But why is it that certain types of people always end up successful and expanding? And others end up on the short end of the stick no matter what advantage they start out with? Even when given the advantage of knowledge, training or experience, the people in the latter group don't seem to be able to apply or use their advantage.

Yet people in the former group mentioned above somehow seem to be able to turn any situation into a win for not only themselves, but those connected with them as well. So, what is the fundamental difference between these two types of people?

The answer has been stated many times in many different ways, but simply, *it's all a state of mind.*

Some people get so involved with *negativity* that this becomes the theme of their lives and the justification and excuse for their failures; it tends to feed on itself and create more of the same.

Successful people also have a pattern of success in their lives. But to fully grasp it, you have to look for a reason that is as simple as it is significant. Successful people have a positive expectancy about their lives.

Whether from nature, nurture, education or training, it's something that is a part of their natural way of thinking and acting. Winners may not always have been on top, but the majority of them *expected* to win.

Once in a great while, by some fluke, someone who never expected to win ends up crossing the finish line first, but this is the exception.

Do you see yourself as a winner or a loser? Either way, your opinion of yourself becomes a self-fulfilling prophecy – a positive expectancy or a negative expectancy.

Which view do you have?

If you're a winner in your own mind, strengthen it. If you see yourself as a loser, take fast action now to change that attitude, using whatever effective method is available.

Your career, your future, and your life depend upon it.

EXPECTATIONS CREATE FUTURES

Once you realize that *your expectations create your future, you're* in the driver's seat of your career and your life. Expectations, imaginations, aspirations and dreams all deal in futures. To the degree you keep these things in mind, your chances of bringing them about are dramatically increased. But, expectations, much like *the sword of truth*, cut both ways.

If you're *expecting to lose*, then this is what will tend to occur. If you expect the worst, that is what is likely to happen. How could it do otherwise when this is all you're looking for?

On the other hand if you are sincerely *expecting to win* you will find it more often than not. For even when you experience a loss, if you approach it with interest and not dismay, you'll stay in control of your expectations and your future. Charles F. Kettering, inventor of the electric starter, gives his viewpoint on expectations:

"High achievement always takes place in the framework of high **expectations."**

As positive expectancy and negative expectancy both thrive on attention, which one you focus on grows stronger.

Selling is a tough profession and only the most persistent survive. Ask yourself; can you *accept* a failure without then *expecting* to fail again? Can you take a loss in stride without changing your attitude about the future?

If so, then you're still in the game and you still have a chance to win.

Legendary basketball star, Michael Jordan reveals one of his secrets to success:

"I've missed more than 9,000 shots in my career. I've lost almost 300 games. 26 times I've been trusted to take the game winning shot and missed.

I've failed over and over and over again in my life. And that is why I succeed. *You have to expect things of yourself before you can do them."*

Periodically take careful inventory of what you are expecting; your future is very definitely influenced by your expectations in the present.

EXTRAORDINARY SERVICE

We're getting numb to it, aren't we? We're so used to getting bad service (meaning *no service*), that too often, we accept it without complaint.

How many times have you had to deal with a bored, apathetic clerk who couldn't care less that you walked out of the store, angrily saying, *"I'll never shop here again,"* while the clerk shrugs and continues with mindless busy-work, without giving you a second thought.

Under these circumstances, even if you are only slightly better than average you will stand out from the crowd. If you're *much better* than average, they will see you as extraordinary. Customers have excellent memories about how they feel. If you make them feel important, they'll always remember it. If you make them feel insignificant, they'll never forget it.

In dealing with or training sales reps, I often ask them this question, *"What did you do today that will make your customers remember you as the best sales rep they've ever dealt with?"*

All too often, I get answers that range from "nothing" to "not much." It's a problem.

It boils down to a matter of handling expectations. If you give people *less than they expected*, they may not say anything to you, but they will silently feel that they just got conned, and that, they do not forget.

You can also be sure that they will mention it to others. If you give people about what they expected (fair business practices), they may be satisfied with the exchange, but nothing to write home about.

The key to extraordinary service is to *give them more than they expected.*

Exceed their expectations and they will never forget that you made them feel important and valuable as a customer. And this is something they will enthusiastically tell others about. Given a choice, they will come back to see you. They will also recommend you to their friends as a problem-solver after the sale. Importantly, they also tend to stay loyal to you forever.

Why? Because you were **interested in helping them** as your top priority.

Your customers want someone they can brag about to their friends. They want you to be the best in the business. They want to know they've got an expert in their corner whenever they need one. They want you to be friendly, efficient, and understanding and effective in handling their problems. But most of all, they want to *feel that they made the right choice* in working with you - someone they can trust. Why not give them what they want?

FACTS TELL - STORIES SELL

People tell me that they drift off if I start talking about facts or figures. It's true that most people do have a limited digestion for a steady diet of facts and figures, preferring a well-told story every time.

American author Brian Morton said it this way:

"The world, the human world, is bound together not by protons and electrons, but by stories."

And, in my opinion, he's right.

The idea saying, facts tell, stories sell, has become a popular sales mantra over the years and the concept is already well known to all successful salespeople. To new salespeople though, the idea is stated like this: *if you must talk, at least tell a good story.*

Okay, so where do you find a good story? You already have more good stories than you can count; you just have to learn to use them.

Here's the three basic parts of a good story:

1. situation or challenge,
2. effort or struggle to overcome the problem,
3. resolution or the answer.

Now, these are the five steps to get you going on the right track.

1. An initial confusion develops, causing a problem conflict (indecision, fear of making a mistake), or challenge

2. A temporary fix is accomplished and things settle down

3. Problem reappears, failed attempts with more confusion, stress and bruised feelings leading to more confusion, more challenges and more failed solutions

4. At last, to everyone's surprise, the true, unexpected, source of the problem is discovered

5. Proper solution is implemented; problem or challenge is dissolved.

The theme should grow out of the story. Don't preach, just tell the story and let the listener figure things out for themselves.

A good story has humanity. Emotions are human. Problems are human, confusions and complexities are human; attempted and failed solutions are human.

Since time immemorial all people have had troubles, worries, stresses, difficulties and problems.

The human emotional connection is the key to a good story. It has to make you feel something.

If it doesn't affect you emotionally, it's forgettable and commonly is out of mind instantly.

Law: If they can't feel it, they won't buy it.

Finally, a good story has to catch your attention. Think about the best stories, movies, TV shows, books, etc., that you've heard, seen or read; what was the first thing that captured your attention?

I'm willing to bet, it was the element of surprise.

It can be a sudden unpredicted change or a startling unexpected twist or turn in the story, or any other unforeseen, mystifying event that appears out of the blue.

The perplexing quality of the surprise is what captures attention and ignites your imagination.

This factor is common in all living things. Mystery, curiosity, some oddity or peculiarity it's the "*What is that*?" phenomena that can't be ignored. People love a mystery, a surprise, something they haven't thought of.

If they can predict how the story is going to end before you get there, it's boring. Surprise them and you'll get and keep their attention. Even when you know these facts, it still requires disciplined practice to tell a good story.

Anybody can recite a set of facts or rattle off statistics or figures and read a power-point slide. This will not surprise anyone. And it won't catch anyone's attention. You want them to be interested in what you're saying?

Surprise them with a good story and you may be surprised with the results.

FOCUS COUNTS

Today was the big meeting, the one we had been waiting and preparing for. We thought we were ready for anything, until we came face to face with the man himself. Ross Perot, a self-made billionaire, seemed bigger than his physical stature.

He entered the room, and there was no doubt about who was in charge. But it was more than that. It was clear that we were there for him, not the reverse.

Ross took command immediately and came right to the point, saying,

"The world wants things done, not excuses. One thing done well is worth a million good excuses."

Followed by, "What can you do for me that I can't already do?" He was all business. There were no polite social niceties or mindless chitchat.

The ball was now in our court to do something to prove our value or the meeting was over. Fast!

Luckily, the head of our sales team was a fast thinker and came up with the winning comeback, saying, "Ross, I'm going to make you a very rich man."

After an uncomfortable silence, Ross laughed out loud. The ice was broken when he said with a smile, "Okay, let's see what you've got." We were just audacious enough to get his attention, and he was ready to listen, at least for now.

He was one of the most successful salesmen in history for a reason and we all learned an important lesson that morning: *Focus counts.*

He never let his attention be distracted by anything that wasn't going to forward his purpose. Clearly, focus was one of the keys to his success. Like all professional buyers, he was not influenced by emotional hot buttons that sway most consumers. His attention was under his control and *focused* on the objective he was after.

Here's what he wanted to know:

"Why should I do business with you over anyone else?"

"Who else have you worked with that can vouch for you?"

"How much do you charge?"

"When can you start?"

With Mr. Perot there was no middle ground, either we had what it took or we didn't. He was both a professional salesman and a professional buyer and could see through any fluff and expose any weaknesses instantly. But, luckily, he could also recognize and acknowledge strength and competence in others when he saw it.

In this situation, we were prepared to step up to the plate and take our best swing, and do it with confidence. We answered his questions and held his attention because we were clear, concise, and focused. In the end, we signed a starter deal, which got us in the door as something we were satisfied with.

We had gotten over the first hurdle. We were doing business with the best and we had pulled it off as intended. And you can do the same.

Focused preparation, planning and foresight and a touch of audacity, combined with a no-nonsense business-like approach will get (and keep) you in the game.

Chapter 4

FOR BETTER OR WORSE

The following quote from Norman Vincent Peale contains wisdom that we can all take to heart:

"The person who sends out positive thoughts activates the world around him positively and draws back to himself positive results."

Your future is definitely influenced by what you're creating today, a concept also stated here by an unknown author:

"I know not what the future holds, but I know who holds the future."

And as I have written elsewhere:

Law: The seeds you are planting today determine your future, for better or for worse.

When thoughts of negativity and failure dominate your thinking, you had better stockpile a ready supply of *excuses, justifications, and explanations* to help you live with your failures. You're going to need them.

Losers expect to lose. It's not an accident. In fact, they're surprised when they don't lose, which, in itself, creates a self-fulfilling prophecy for their future. When you give any attention at all to what you can't do or why something can't be done, you make this concept stronger. And, by definition, there is less room for any positive thinking to occur. Here are a few examples of negative thinking:

"Nothing ever turns out the way I want anyway."

"I expect the worst, so I'm never disappointed".

"Oh well, I guess I'm just unlucky, it's fate."

Winners expect to succeed. It's not an accident. And they're not all that surprised when they do win. They did *expect* to be in the spotlight or the winner's circle after all.

They also plan for it with focused practice and preparation. They see and feel themselves as winners and act that way in all their thoughts and feelings. Positive expectancy for the future dominates their thinking and their actions. This alone can become a self-reinforcing prediction of their future.

Their attention is always on attaining the goal; every action they take moves them closer to attainment. Obstacles, barriers, and reasons why *it can't be done* just don't exist in their thinking. They always expect to win, and mostly, they do.

Of course, this *attitude of positivity* includes others in their success.

Dr. Wayne W. Dyer states it this way:

Law: *"The state of your life is nothing more than a reflection of your state of mind."*

You can sense and feel it when you're around someone with a positive attitude. Even when they don't aspire to a lofty position or great wealth, they exude a vibration of positivity that is uplifting and attractive to others.

Want to know which side of the fence you're on? Ask yourself these questions:

What do you think about most of the time?

What do you really expect to happen?

If you are positive in your expectations most of the time, then strengthen this attitude. If your expectations are mostly negative, then something needs to change.

Whatever your response, you're better off knowing where you stand. Accept the challenge and move ahead. If you need a nudge to get you started, here are a few tips:

Exercise, move the body, decide to take a walk every day, if you can't walk, then go in the back yard and throw a ball. Look at things, talk to people, get interested and notice people and things. Eat healthier foods; knock off things and people you know are bad for you.

Why do simple things such as moving the body or extroverting attention help replace anxiety and worry with a better outlook? Research has shown that the human mind can only perform one task at a time.

By directing your attention as you choose, your thoughts and emotions follow suit, leaving worry and stress in the past. You were not born with a *negative attitude* about yourself, others, or life in general. It's not a natural state of mind, and it's not a *life sentence without possibility of parole.* You can change your attitudes and your conditions in life.

As a side note, when you're up to it, take a cold, hard look at the people you associate with. Are they winners or losers? Sometimes what you find will shock you.

This quote from American-Canadian writer William Gibson, will give you something to consider:

"Before you diagnose yourself with depression or low self-esteem, first make sure that you are not, in fact, just surrounded by assholes."

Start with little changes in the right direction that begin a positive habit. Make sure your thoughts and actions in the present align with your **future expectations** and you'll be on your way to living on the positive side of the ledger for a change.

LEVERAGE YOUR EXPECTATIONS

Why is it that no matter what obstacle life throws at them, some people always seem to end up with a positive result? Others, even when given the advantage of superior knowledge, better training or more experience, just never seem to pull it off. What's up with this anyway?

My long-time friend, Cary Kilner, Ph.D., chemist, and educator, proffers an answer. He states,

"When you maintain a high bar, it keeps you striving for the peak of competence and production, and sets a good example for others."

I agree. He has lived this way all his life, at least for the 40+ years we have known each other. No matter what the activity, he maintains a healthy balance of dedication, discipline, and insouciance, making sure he holds the high bar of expectations he sets for himself. You could even say, correctly, that Dr. C.K. is *leveraging his expectations* to create the future he wants.

Here's how it works.

You want something in the future. So you plan, organize and work for it today, with the expectation that the future will reward you with what you want. You are *leveraging your expectations*, your willingness to plan, organize and work today for some betterment or advantage in the future. Even with something as obvious as eating, this still holds true. You want to eat tomorrow, so you work today.

This is a particularly relevant concept for any salesperson. You should conduct a side check from time to time to make sure your expectations are not *holding you back*, as they can have an enormous effect on your future for better or for worse.

When you **expect to win today**, this attitude creates a state of mind that creates the state of your life, now and in the future.

Leveraging your positive expectations creates an infectious confidence that helps bring you closer to your goals in the future.

GATES OF TRUST

It's a time-honored principle: before the prospect will even think about buying anything, they have to know you and trust you.

There is no scarcity of books that talk about lack of trust being one of the first obstacles to any sale, and they are correct. But it's one thing to identify the problem, and another to show you the correct way to handle it. Continue reading and all will be revealed.

Most people use a graduated gate system to sort out the trustworthy from the unworthy. Each gate represents a test, which narrows the pool of applicants and acts as a sort of virus protection for our lives. I have identified five gates that have to be opened to have any chance of getting the prospect to trust you.

Gate One

The first gate is that you must *establish agreement.* This means having something in common with the people you are talking to. Having values and interests that are similarly aligned with your client is an easy way to open this gate.

People tend to trust people who agree with them and with whom they agree. Agreement underlies all successful personal relationships, especially applicable to the field of selling.

Gate Two

The next gate evolves directly from the first: Can they *identify with you*? Do you both *speak the same language*, literally and figuratively? Do you sound like they sound or dress like they dress? This is important, as we tend to identify with people we like and who are like us.

Any talented or charismatic person can adjust their communication style to match the personality of whomever they are trying to persuade. That can mean being more businesslike with someone who likes to cut to the chase, or avoiding too much shoptalk with a more gregarious person.

Charisma doesn't have to be overtly *in your face* – in fact, mostly it's not. A soft-spoken or mild-mannered personality can be considered charismatic, as long as people identify with it. Personal magnetism and a quiet confidence or an understated aura of capability will both put the client at ease.

Effortless competence radiates and attracts people to you far more than the fellow who seems desperate to make the next sale.

Gate Three

The third gate is obvious. Are you are *interested* in them more than you are in yourself? People have a special sense that can detect the presence or absence of this quality. And they can do it instantly. The gate either opens or it remains closed depending more on what they feel than what you say. Being genuinely interested is the key to opening this gate.

Gate Four

The fourth gate is *performance*. Can you *deliver what you promise?* Once established, this not only maintains trust, but it can also lead to new referrals. If you or your company has the reputation of being able to deliver what you promise, clients come to you willingly.

Gate Five

Okay; hold your hat because this one may surprise you. I have saved it for last, but arguably it could have been first, it is that important, as it must be in place before you start to work on any of the other gates. Here it is: *You must like and trust yourself first.*

Once you have this one firmly under your belt, you've hit the jackpot. If you are worthy of trust, people will also tend to trust you.

There is no greater way to engender the trust of others than to start with the ability to like and trust yourself first. Learn these five gates well and you'll be happy you did. So will your customers.

CHARGING WHAT YOU'RE WORTH

What you're worth can vary widely based upon location, timing, competition, and other circumstances. In theory there should be no difference between what you're paid and what you're worth. In practice, there is.

A legendary story about automaker, Henry Ford, holds that he once had a problem with the generators in his factory. He hired electrical genius, Charlie Steinmetz, to figure out the problem, which he did, and Ford received a bill for $10,000 (an enormous sum in those days).

Steinmetz broke down the outrageous price:

1. 1. It cost $10 to tinker with the generators.
2. 2. $9,990 for a lifetime *of learning how to tinker.*

Ford paid the bill, happily.

In another famous example, Pablo Picasso was sketching in the park when a bold woman approached him, saying, "It's you —Picasso, the great artist! Oh, you must sketch my portrait! I insist."

So Picasso agreed to sketch her. After studying her for a moment, he used a single pencil stroke to create her portrait.

As he handed the women his work of art, she gushed,

"It's perfect! You managed to capture my essence with one stroke, in one moment. Thank you! How much do I owe you?"

"Five thousand dollars," the artist replied. "B-b-but, what? She sputtered. How could you want so much money for this picture? It only took you a second to draw it!" To which Picasso responded, "Madame, it took me my entire life."

The lesson? From the client point of view, the value of a product or service is how much they need it right now! Just don't put yourself in a situation where you devalue or underestimate the value of your skills and services in the marketplace just because you can get the job done quickly or need the money.

So, what is the worth of a product or service? The perceived value of the service is determined by how much it is needed and wanted right now, with how much it is *wanted* taking top priority.

Charge an amount approximately equivalent to how much it is wanted and needed. But not too much so that it is outside any possibility of them paying for it.

GREATNESS IN SELLING

I love the feeling from a jolt of creativity hitting me when I least expect it. Especially when accompanied by a bolt of inspiration; exactly what happened to me.

Many years ago, on a flight returning to Los Angeles from the East coast, I was working on my computer, trying to finish a new sales article. A passenger next to me noticed what I was writing and commented that he too was involved in sales. I looked over as he started to introduce himself and exclaimed,

"Wait a minute, you're Tom Hopkins, of course I know who you are," I said, just loud enough to interest even the passengers back in coach. Indulging my excitement, he politely accepted my compliment and we proceeded to have a pleasant and enlightening conversation. I had read his first book, *How to Master the Art of Selling* and explained that I had established a

hugely successful, international sales force based upon the principles outlined in his books.

I was struck by the fact that not only was he **friendly** and open, he was also **sincerely interested** in everything I had to say. This alone caused me to be more interested in him and what he was saying. Our brief encounter confirmed for me why he is so successful in his chosen profession as a salesman and author.

I also noticed one important thing: he *sounds like he writes and writes like he talks* – just by being himself.

It was in that instant that I realized what made him a sales master: he was able to get me to like him and trust him instantly, while doing nothing else than just being himself; what's more it seemed effortless, without any stress, strain or effort.

He was *just being himself.*

He also demonstrated the truth of one of the most basic secrets to sales greatness: *Being yourself and being sincerely interested is the first step to sales greatness.*

So, here they are, the secrets of sales greatness:

1. Be yourself.
2. Be sincerely interested.
3. Know, understand, and apply the fundamentals.
4. Develop your own personal methods.
5. Practice until you can't do it wrong.

Now it's yours, to understand, practice and prosper.

GOT ATTITUDE?

Has this ever happened to you? You're determined to get the best value for your money and not get talked into buying something you don't want - but the salesperson has other ideas.

Far too often you run into a sales rep that falls into one of these categories:

1. The one who, because of their experience or job title they think they *know best* about what is right for you before you've said a word.

2. The one with an air of slick confidence who makes you feel like you're being seduced into buying something *you didn't need or want.*

3. The one whose outlook, approach, sincerity and interest convey the confidence that *they're looking out for your best interests first.*

Which one would you rather deal with, even if it were not the lowest price? Which one would you refer to your friends?

Many customers base their purchasing decisions on how they *feel* around the salesperson. And this is something they never forget. You can talk endlessly about features, advantages and benefits of your product or service but it will fall on deaf ears unless they have decided you're worth listening to.

Only when you have a positive place in the customer's mind, will what you're offering get at least a fair hearing.

For example, my wife and I walked into a local camera store, the old-school style that looked like it had been there forever – old cameras were stacked everywhere, obviously loved by the owner.

That person would likely appreciate anyone with similar interests – a fact that was unfortunately overlooked by the sales clerk of the day.

My wife was carrying an expensive Nikon camera, which should have conveyed interest in quality, but the clerk, oblivious to us, engaged in reading something about computer games, didn't even notice. A friendly greeting on our part was met with an attitude of mild annoyance and disinterest, apparently because we interrupted the atmosphere of tomb-like, motionless silence in the store. The clerk's response to a polite question about the availability of a bulb for an enlarger was to bark a hostile remark that they didn't have it.

I tried again. *"You have a lot of great cameras here, and someone obviously put a lot of time into acquiring them. Do you like cameras?"* Her unintelligible grunt was no help. I tried again. *"Are you the owner of this place"?* No response.

Well, okay then. We got the message - as we quickly looked for the door - she considered our presence there as an intrusion. This twenty-something clerk had an **attitude,** for sure. And it wasn't friendly.

It wasn't exactly the best approach to sell anything but unfortunately this situation is very common these days. It appears that disinterest and disservice have become the norm rather than the exception.

It is a natural law of selling that a friendly, positive attitude is the *most important quality* you can develop as a salesperson. Your attitude either opens doors for you or *ensures they will stay shut.*

Unfortunately, this is not something you acquire in institutions of higher learning. For some reason, the current educational trend seems to focus on mastering technical skills and attaining good grades, while ignoring people skills. Somewhere along the line, the *human element* in the equation got lost. In fact, however, a friendly, welcoming attitude, along with honesty and trust, are the most useful principles and values you can develop as a professional salesperson. These will open doors to relationships and future sales more than any other significant factor.

INVISIBLE SENSE AWARENESS

It's free; maybe that's why we take it for granted; but if you do, you're wasting a valuable resource.

What is it? It's *your invisible sense awareness* - that ability to perceive by the senses, rather than just by the intellect.

These are methods by which you become aware of and perceive what is happening around you, by direct observation, insight, intuition or other means. The word *perception* itself implies *consciousness*; something, too often, in short supply.

Senses are hidden from the view, yet we can easily perceive their effects. *Common sense* is an example. It's native to any person, yet invisible to the naked eye.

Commonly, we think of only five senses: *sight, smell, touch, hearing, and taste.* Research, however, has added a few more such as: pain, tempera-ture, balance, joint motion and acceleration, time and many others.

The art and craft of selling incorporates all the sense perceptions, invis-ible or not. As any professional salesperson can testify, you can often sense what is going on with a prospect, often much sooner than expected. Some come by this ability innately, others by careful training and long experience.

It is similar to the experienced hunter who can sense danger, long before anyone else, by the *absence* of usual, subtle noises; or the customs agent at the border, checking luggage for contraband who can sense that someone is hiding something just by the way *it feels* or the way they look; or the experienced doctor who can tell a serious injury from a minor one by subtle indicators missed by the casual observer.

These people are using their experience and instinctive invisible sense awareness to their best advantage. And the more they use it, the stronger and more refined it becomes. So it is with selling.

Using your *invisible and visible* sense awareness is a practiced ability that grows stronger with experience and use. Inexperienced sales people often resort to crude, sophomoric questions like, "*Are you feeling stressful about this deal?*" (causing even more stress in the prospect). The sales master, drawing on years of experience, instincts and sense awareness – is able to subtly *adjust any selling procedure or method to the client.*

In this manner, they can defuse small problems before they develop into big issues and keep the client on track. You can begin to do the same by being aware of and trusting your instincts and by strengthening your **invisible sense awareness.**

Practicing the following three steps will help:

1. First, become aware that *invisible sense perceptions* do exist.
2. Next, begin to *wake up your senses* by practicing them every day; focusing on one perception at a time. Even a one-minute practice of the five traditional senses, touch, sight, smell, taste and hearing, can make a dramatic change for the better.
3. The third and most important step is to make the decision to *trust your senses.*

Rather than negating, dismissing or ignoring the signals you are receiving from your sense perceptions, become aware of them and begin to **trust** them.

If, more times than you like, you find yourself thinking, "I knew I should have ... " or, "I wish I had trusted my instincts,"- you are not trusting the natural savvy you were born with.

Recognize that *common sense* is something we're all born with, as it is with all the other senses. But too often our common sense is trumped by justifications, rationalizations, excuses or contrary opinions from others.

As you become aware of and trust both the visible and *the invisible senses – the stronger they become. And their natural power* begins to become far more useful.

Your sense perceptions grow stronger with use, and weaker with neglect. They are there for your use to give you that edge you need to put you ahead of the competition. Like any other ability, it grows strong with exercise and atrophies from disuse.

IS CHANGE THE ONLY CONSTANT?

His opening statement caught me by surprise, likely due to being still stuck in my usual early-morning fog.

"There is only one predictable constant in nature and in life, and that is change," said the professor. But I silently puzzled, "Wait a minute, how could change be a constant?" With an air of finality, he declared,

"Nothing stays the same, except this fact. In the physical universe, change is not only constant, it's inevitable." It didn't look like he was about to say it again. Thankfully, it wasn't necessary, as his words finally sunk in.

He was talking about the *physical universe*; and since we all live in a universe that is in constant motion, then obviously change really is the only constant.

I got the wake-up call I needed and a dim bulb of enlightenment began to glow through the thickets of significance in my freshman brain. That epiphany altered my perception of life in some very exciting ways. The professor smiled with knowing and obvious delight at our recognition of the basic truth that change is not only something we must accept. But it also is something to *embrace* and use to our advantage.

Professor Mandelstam was one of the most highly respected Economics Professors at Michigan State University, where I was enrolled as an intrepid student many years ago. He taught a beginning economics class in a huge lecture hall, putting on an engaging and entertaining performance with each lecture.

I'm certain he would be proud to learn that the fact of my realizing this basic principle of the inevitability of change became a *stabilizing influence* in my life.

For when I realized that nothing stays the same in a universe that is in constant motion, I also recognized that n*egative change is not permanent*, and *positive change* was not only possible, but under certain circumstances, entirely plausible. I also began to see that there just might be something I could do to bring about a change in the direction I wanted.

While I thank the learned professor for introducing me to the basic principle of the inevitability of change, he failed to mention one other important point that I consider key to the whole subject:

Law: External change follows internal change.

This fundamental principle is as powerful as any other, perhaps even more. The most effective way to create internal change around you is to first **change your attitude.**

Your mental outlook will act as a predisposition to influence a positive or negative outcome for your future. Whether you to *expect to win or lose,* depends to no small degree upon your attitude.

The discovery that **change starts with me**, put me in the driver's seat of my life and has done more to create a positive outlook than anything else I have studied or experienced. If I ever found myself shipwrecked along with other flotsam and jetsam on the shoals of existence with no hope of rescue, all I had to do was *not let the circumstances of life determine my attitude.*

And that *inevitability of change* also meant that I could change things for the better too. As a result, failure never affects me for long if I remember to change my own attitude first.

IS FAILURE REALLY THE BEST TEACHER?

Bill Gates, American business magnate, former chief executive officer and current chairman of Microsoft, was quoted as saying the following about success and failure: "Success is a lousy teacher. It seduces smart people into thinking they can't lose."

This is a concept shared by acclaimed Scottish author, Samuel Smiles – the father of the self-help movement in 1855 with his self-published book, *Self-Help* – an instant best seller, elevating him to celebrity status almost overnight. Here are some of his thoughts on the subject of success and failure.

"It is a mistake to suppose that men succeed through success; they much oftener succeed through failures. We learn wisdom from failure much more than from success . . . he who never made a mistake, never made a discovery."

I agree. For when able individuals fail, they can catch their breath, dust themselves off, look at why it happened, learn from their mistakes, correct them and do better in the future. However, when some people succeed, often they believe they have found the secret to endless success and don't even bother to examine what they did to achieve it.

So, inevitably, when they do fail at some future point, they are without hope of change, as they don't know why they failed.

I would much rather have someone in my corner who had been through the pain of failure and who then got back on their feet armed with the wisdom of what went wrong and how to fix it so it didn't happen again.

Please note: I'm not suggesting that you engage in reckless behavior. The difference between a calculated, considered risk and reckless irresponsibility is huge.

But when I find someone who is willing to take a calculated risk on a chance that could result in huge advances forward, this person is far more valuable to me when the chips are down.

Simply, I don't trust someone who brags about the fact that they have *never failed or never lost money.* They will eventually, and usually it is your money that will pay for their inexperience.

I'd always rather have someone on my side who has the battle scars of life and who has learned from their mistakes.

Failure can indeed be a better teacher than success, but only if you learn from those mistakes so as not to repeat them.

Never be afraid to make mistakes. The only people who never make mistakes are those who are not in the game.

A failure is not a man who has once stumbled. Rather, it is a man who stumbles and who *is unwilling to use* the experience to his advantage in the future.

George Bernard Shaw agrees:

"A life spent making mistakes is not only more honorable, but more useful than a life spent doing nothing."

I've often said that *life is a contact sport* - and I still hold firm to this idea. Take your wins and your losses in stride and continue on with a light-hearted attitude toward accomplishment.

For as often as not, the challenges thrown your way will turn out better than you thought they would anyway.

Thrive on challenge, risk and the adventure of active involvement in life, and always **expect to win** and take close inventory of what occurred if you don't.

This quote by Jack Nicholson, as R.P. McMurphy, in the 1975 movie, *One Flew Over The Cuckoo's Nest,* illustrates the point as well as any I've seen.

While incarcerated in a mental institution after failing to escape by throwing a sink through a window, he said to the others watching him,

"But I tried, didn't I? Goddamnit, at least I did that."

I'd always prefer to be around people who tried; and if they failed, got up, dusted themselves off, and tried again. Failure is not a life sentence. It really is a better teacher – if, instead of avoiding it, you let it help you and use it to your advantage.

IT'S NOT PERSONAL – or is it?

"It's nothing personal; it's just business." Ever heard this?

If you have, it was most likely said just before you lost that big account you were sure was in the bag, or received a pink slip unexpectedly.

This adage is used most often only when the person saying it is trying to *justify the bad things* they've done (or about to do), that they're not particularly proud of.

The truth is, in sales, in business or in life, *the phrase is not true.* In fact, there is a law about this.

Law: Selling is always personal.

Why? Because no matter how many people are involved in the sale, at the end of the day, you're always selling to an individual person.

Techniques and methods can and do change, but the basic, fundamental laws of dealing with people never change. If you build your selling strategy on the bedrock of understanding people first, you'll find yourself able to best the challenges from any changing business environment.

In sales, it is never just business – because selling is always personal.

JUST TELL THE TRUTH

You're unlikely to find this sales tip in other books on selling. But believe me, this is worth its weight in gold. Basic truths and fundamental principles do exist in the profession of selling. Such truths can be called *natural laws* because they are as powerful and predictable as the laws of nature.

If you know and can use these laws, you gain an advantage over those who don't know.

And this one is a winner: **Just tell the truth**.

If a working definition for truth is *something that works, this one definitely fits the bill.* When everything else fails, *just telling the truth will* often *cut the Gordian knot* (disentangle an impossibly complex circumstance) of any thorny situation.

It simplifies complexities and gets you out of more messes, tough spots and delicate situations than you can imagine. Also, it's far easier to remember what you said than trying to keep track of lies.

Living with truth gives you control, influence and persuasiveness beyond your wildest expectations.

Here's a personal example:

I was a greenhorn salesman sitting in front of the prospective customer, inwardly nervous while outwardly trying to put up a good front, as the prospect was more experienced in sales than I. So, I decided to come clean and lay the truth on the line.

Here is what I said,

"I'm not a salesman; I don't know anything about selling. But I know how to get things done. And I'm also as certain as I have ever been that I can get you want you want, when you want it. What's more, I will work harder than anyone to make sure it happens."

Evidently, my candor surprised him as I got his attention, his interest, and I got the sale. I also learned a valuable and important lesson that day: to get someone's attention, *tell the truth and they'll never forget you.* Why? Because truth has a power and simplicity to it that cuts through lies, deception, and slick sales patter.

Just tell the truth instead of searching for lame excuses, and poor explanations and unconvincing justifications and you'll cut through the complexities that inevitably surround all lies. Many great thinkers agree:

Law: "Honesty and integrity are absolutely essential for success in life – all areas of life." – Zig Ziglar

"Integrity is telling myself the truth. And honesty is telling the truth to other people." - Spencer Johnson, M.D., bestselling author

"Anyone who doesn't take truth seriously in small matters cannot be trusted in large ones either". – Albert Einstein

"Live truth instead of professing it."– Elbert Hubbard, best-selling author, philosopher.

No person has a monopoly on truth. It is freely available to all who care to search for it. Further, you'll know it when you hear it.

Law: Truth knows no borders, answers to no authority and is owned by no one individual. It rings as clear as a bell, shines like Mars at Perihelion, is ubiquitous, immutable, undeniable and virtually *unstoppable.*

Chapter 5

KEEP IT SIMPLE

Once again, the great Ralph Waldo Emerson duplicates my sentiments on this subject perfectly:

"Nothing astonishes men so much as common sense and plain dealing."

While this idea is not new, it is still true.

This concept can apply to any time in history, but especially in today's cultural and economic environment with common sense and plain dealing in very short supply.

As a sales executive, to make an impression, your message must embody at least these two things:

1. A clear vision of the message you are trying to communicate
2. A healthy dose of *common sense and plain dealing.*

Speaking with clarity, simplicity, and brevity will separate you from the crowd and leave them wanting more. But, what you say is often less important than how you say it.

If you come across like you're lecturing, talking down to the customer, bragging, or overly pushy, your message will fall on deaf ears.

There is a way to avoid this. These points are worth considering at least as a starting point:

Clarify your own purposes. Why are you selling?

Identify your product. What are you selling?

Why is your product different than others?

Contact people. Who is your individual customer?

Simplify what you're saying. What is your message?

Focus on one idea at a time. Don't mix messages.

Expectations are vital. What do you expect to achieve?

Underneath all the techniques and methods of selling it is as simple as this:

"Nothing is more simple than greatness; indeed, to be simple is to be great."

And Ralph Waldo Emerson's words above are echoed by Steve Jobs when he said:

"You have to work hard to get your thinking clean to make it simple."

I couldn't agree more.

ARE YOU IMPRESSING OR EXPRESSING?

What are you really trying to do?

Impress them with how much you know?

Or *express* your message, briefly, clearly and *move them into action*?

You already know more about what you're selling than they need to know to make a buying decision and they don't really need to know all that stuff. Keep your priorities in order when speaking and you'll make more sales. This short story might give you a ready reminder.

A young salesman was invited to give a presentation to a large group for the first time, so he approached his mentor for advice about giving a good speech.

The older man came up with some gemstones:

"First of all, *the more you talk the less they remember. To give an unforgettable, compelling presentation, follow these three steps.*

1. *1. Write an exciting opening to capture the attention of everyone in your audience.*
2. *2. Next, write a dramatic, compelling summary to spark the imagination and move people to action.*
3. *3. Finally, put these two steps as* close together *as possible."*

Law: The more you talk, the less they remember.

LIKE YOURSELF FIRST

It's the first thing people notice about you and it happens without speaking a word - but what you're projecting speaks volumes – *loudly.* What is it? It's your **attitude about yourself** – something that you're broadcasting to others all the time – for better or worse.

Your feelings of certainty, competence, and confidence (or uncertainty, inexperience and fear of failure) influence other people more than you might suspect.

Do you love your job, or hate it? Like people? Distrust people? Either way, it shows, and others are affected positively or negatively by these feelings. Your attitudes are determined by your personal opinions and feelings about yourself, others, your job and your life in general.

Other people perceive each of these attitudes and more, every time you interact with them. The message comes across through your posture, your eyes, tone of voice, your manner, what you say and how you say it, your general outlook on life and other less visible elements.

As most people base their feelings about you on first impressions, your attitude about yourself takes on a vital role. Whether they like you or not is directly proportional to how much you like and trust yourself.

There is a powerful element at work here and it can propel you to stellar heights or sabotage your best efforts at getting ahead: If you don't like you they will tend to follow your lead.

Law: If you don't trust you, why should anyone else?

Trust is the glue that holds personal relationships together; if they don't like or trust you, people will search out or invent reasons to avoid being around you. So what can you do if you're not feeling that great about yourself today? Here are a few tips that might help get your attitude on the right track.

First, just imagine that you have something to smile about. Then force yourself to smile for at least one minute. Yes, just smile. I know, it may seem a little artificial at first, but soon you'll find it's easier to do without effort.

Next, find something that you like or admire about yourself, your job, your house, your friends, your life, or anything at all. Keep at it for at least one minute or until you feel a change for the better.

Finally, get outside and **talk to people – get interested in people** and you'll see that they're interested in you. Just ask them something that you might be interested in. Ask them about their business, the weather, the price of gas, anything. You'll see they're not that scary. Just keep at this until you feel at least a little better.

It only takes a very slight change to create a huge difference in the way you are perceived by others.

The result is that you will attract more attention, interest, friends and relationships; and soon you really will have something to smile about.

LISTEN, LEARN, LEAD

By definition, new ideas appear unexpectedly, and this one is no exception. It's a concept rooted in one of the oldest doctrines of selling - *learn to listen - listen to learn* – but with a fresh new twist.

I discovered this one from reading a speech by a public figure who opened a meeting with this statement:

"I came here to listen, to learn and to lead."

With this simple, powerful opening statement he repositioned himself in the minds of his audience. He was no longer just a professorial lecturer or professional speaker; instead, he placed himself *in the role of the student.*

He was open and ready to *listen and learn*, a far more acceptable role to any audience, effectively side stepping any embedded resistance or fixed assumptions that may have existed. Most importantly, he did this by adding a simple element of surprise to what they already knew.

If you're not already familiar with it, the phrase, *learn to listen, and listen to learn* is a good one to know and use.

But adding the third step to the process as in *listen, learn, and lead,* turns it into the perfect tool for any selling activity, as simple as it is powerful.

Each one of these three concepts depend on the other two. What makes them unique is their interdependency when used in the order listed. Sometimes it's easier to understand if you look at it in reverse.

You can't *lead* the prospect where you want them to go unless you first *learn* where they want to go. Also, it's impossible to discover what their problems are unless are you *listen to them first.*

If you ask questions designed to interest the client, engage their attention and stimulate his or her imagination, then listen to what they say, you're on the right path. This way you can learn what they really want and need and you can then lead them to a point where they realize the benefit of doing business with you.

While there is no guarantee that any sales tool will work in every situation, I can assure you of one thing: omitting any one of these three ingredients will guarantee that *you will lose the sale.*

Law: Learn to listen, listen to learn.

WHAT DO THEY *REALLY* WANT?

Why are there always deals that slip away at the last second, after you've seemingly done everything right?

After all, you've contacted, connected, communicated with and engaged the customer; you've qualified them, clarified their purposes, answered their questions, and handled objections. You've even got them to agree that they *need* what you're offering.

But when their response is something like this, I get a bad feeling. I know I missed something.

"Thank you. I know everyone enjoyed your presentation."

"Very impressive, it's obvious that you know your material."

"What you say makes a lot of sense. Let me think it over and get back to you."

These are polite, logical, and reasoned statements, usually followed by a quick customer departure and no commitment. You're left scratching your head in disbelief, wondering, "What did I miss?"

The problem is this: you may be selling what you think they need, but *not what they know they want.*

The fundamental principle underlying this concept is simple and powerful:

Law: *What they want to buy* is more important than *what you want to sell.*

Unless they *need* and also *want it*, they'll always try to kick the can down the road and find a reason to put off buying what you're selling.

The question to ask yourself is: *What do they really want?* You may assume you've changed their minds with reasoning and rational thought, but there's almost no chance that you'll change their *innermost feelings.* Why? Because what they *really want* is rooted in feelings and emotions, not thinking or logic.

The classic mistake many sales people make is to try to motivate people to action with logic, facts and figures. But it doesn't work that way; in fact, it's just the reverse.

Law: If they can't see it, they won't believe it.

And if they don't believe it, they won't buy it.

But once they do see a *personal benefit or advantage* in what you're offering, the emotional temperature will rise high enough to create the motivation to buy. Once that happens, they use the logic and rationale to support their belief that it is the right thing to do.

What they feel is the *key factor* in creating a decision.

If you present the logical elements with a *human touch* that aligns with what they really want, you're building an emotional bridge that can lead to a close.

THE CART BEFORE THE HORSE

"I just focus on making a friend before I even think about making a sale," he said, when I asked my friend for his secret to success in selling.

And this simple formula has worked for him his whole career. It is something we can all use to better advantage. New sales people, unfortunately, tend to focus on *what words to say* to get more sales; a perfect example of putting the cart before the horse, a phrase in Greek is called "hysteron proteron" or *latter before*.

In the early days of door-to-door selling there was a common slogan to remind the reps of the proper order of things in selling: "You have to open the door, to make a sale," and the way you open the door is to make a friend before you start selling.

They also knew that every sale is different. Just because the last one closed easily, doesn't mean the next one will. Also every sale has a pace that aligns with the customer. This is the natural order of selling.

But reverse this natural order and it's like trying to get your cat to sit on your lap when they don't want to; it just doesn't work.

In dealing with people, you can never predict with 100% accuracy exactly what they will do. But, you can always count on one thing: inverting the natural order of actions or ideas will inevitably lead to frustration for both you and the prospect that can squelch any deal.

Then, when this happens, the tendency is to resort to *force selling* (bullying the client to buy). And this is something that always comes back to bite you.

So why not do it the easy way?

Make a friend before you make a sale. Your prospect will be happier with the process, and so will you. It's always good to keep the customer satisfied.

MARKETING VERSUS SALES

I suppose the title really could be marketing plus sales as both areas are vital to expect to succeed in business.

Sales people have to rely on marketing to do its job of promoting a product or service to the public generally. And marketing people must rely on the sales people to carry the ball to the individual customer and close the deals that that began as a marketing plan.

These two elements are two sides of the same coin and share equal importance. But, in spite of the symbiotic, mutually beneficial relationship between the two, differences can arise. Why? Because the focus of marketing is *on the product*, while sales is focused *on the people*.

The orientation of sales generally and selling specifically requires attention on *the individual customer* through building client relationships, developing new accounts and servicing ongoing accounts, getting referrals and immediate or future sales. Compensation and promotions come from *direct or indirect sales* results.

Marketing has its emphasis on *the specific product line,* building long-term market actions, maximizing individual product line profitability, which may include balancing the product portfolio, and discontinuing less profitable products.

Marketing is compensated and promoted on *longer-term product line goals.*

Why is this distinction important? Because it is the salesperson's job to contact the individual, and ultimately ask for the order and get the check. This is up close and personal and something that marketing never has to face. If, as a salesman or woman, you are not up to this aspect of your job, marketing might be a better fit for you.

While marketing faces other important challenges, coming *face to face* with the individual buyer is not one of them. This is solely the role of those directly involved in selling. Each, however, play an important role in accomplishing the overall goals. Without marketing, sales results would suffer and without sales, marketing would likely fail.

Ideally, they work together to share knowledge, areas of competency, and the same overall objectives and purposes with attention on the long-term goals.

Even with the one-man-show operations, there is still marketing AND sales.

You have to do both jobs and more to succeed in the long run, whether in a large, multi-layered corporation or an entrepreneur starting out on your own. Selling involves personal relationships with the individual customer. Marketing deals with the dynamic of people in general. Learn to celebrate the differences between sales and marketing and savor the benefits of the similarities and you'll win in both the short and the long run.

Law: Market to people, sell to the individual.

MISSION CRITICAL

When I'm working with salespeople to debug a thorny sale in process, I always ask this question:

"Tell me about the people first, then we'll handle the sale."

Long, hard-won experience has taught me one simple truth.

When you run into trouble on a step of the sales procedure, *you skipped an earlier step* or didn't fully complete it. Most often, you failed to really contact and make a *connection with the individual before you tried to sell them anything. As the old saying correctly states: the customer always comes first.*

We don't live in a totalitarian dictatorship, where people are forced to buy something even if they don't need it or want it . . . at least not yet.

But no matter what sales **method**, technique, tactic, or system you are using, you will always have trouble unless you keep this in mind: business is second – people come first.

If you try to skip this step of handling the people first, or rush through it so you can close the deal fast, it will come back to bite you!

Why make *trouble* for yourself unnecessarily?

Spend as much time as needed to fully handle the people first, this will always make the business side of things go much, much smoother. They'll feel better about the purchase and you'll feel better about the sale.

If you only learn one thing from this article, this law is *mission-critical*:

Law: Handle the people first, business second.

MIXED MESSAGES INDIGESTION

I once worked with a dynamic individual who was convinced she could sell anything to anybody. Mostly, she was right; but she had one weakness. By trying to sell more than one idea at a time, she ended up giving the client a bad case of *mixed messages indigestion*.

You'll see examples of this all the time with marketing and selling products or services such as, "Oil Change and Tanning Booth" (while you wait); or "Landscaping Services and Dental Cleaning" or "High-Tech Marketing Services and Burial Insurance."

These are obviously gags. But mixing messages can leave people walking away, confused and scratching their heads about what you're selling. People have a limited digestion for too many ideas or messages at the same time.

Law: Most people can absorb only one idea at a time.

If your presentation allows them to grasp one idea after another in logical, sequential fashion, they'll follow you to your conclusion. Otherwise, you'll lose them and you'll end up with nothing.

The recipe for failure is to give your presentation on a product or service and also include a pitch for a donation to your favorite charity.

Don't do it. Why? Because you're *mixing messages.*

Example: I once used an accountant, a competent CPA, who abruptly changed his career path. He decided he wanted to become a consultant and make the big bucks!

So, he began a promotional campaign to build this business while also continuing his accounting business. Ultimately, he failed. Because clients no longer knew who or what they were hiring.

He was confusing his customers; and confused customers can't decide one way or the other.

Stick to one idea at a time. Be known as the expert at that one thing first. Own that territory and drive home your own unique message. Don't try to be everything to everybody and you'll avoid creating mixed messages indigestion in your prospects. If you give them too much at once, you'll lose their attention and interest and you'll also lose the sale.

The watchword is to keep a consistent focused message. You have to keep an eye on this during every customer interaction.

Failing to maintain a consistent, focused message is one of the most common mistakes made by salespeople - important enough in fact to fall in the category of a basic law of selling:

Law: Mixed messages create a confused customer.

A confused customer can't decide. If the customer *can't decide, they won't buy.*

MY "AH-HA" MOMENT

This was it, my "ah-ha" moment. It came when I was reading something that literally jumped off the page and stopped me in my tracks.

Here it is:

"As to methods there may be a million and then some, but principles are few. The man who grasps principles can successfully select his own methods. The man who tries methods, ignoring principles, is sure to have trouble."

In these few words **Ralph Waldo Emerson** stated exactly what I had searched for my whole life to discover the basic principles and laws underlying all life and living, then finding methods of applying those principles that work for me.

This realigned and clarified many cloudy areas of my life and I believe a careful reading may do the same for you.

First, let's break down the three main elements of this writing by Mr. Emerson.

1. "As to methods there may be a million and then some, but principles are few." Translation: When your methods reinforce your principles – your principles empower your methods. Both are critical to everything you do in the sales profession as they make up the woof and warp – or the underlying structure – of all successful sales actions and activities.

2. "The man who grasps principles can successfully select his own methods." Methods are HOW. Principles are WHY. There are many routes (methods) to success if methods do not violate your principles because they are synergetic and depend on each other for workability.

3. "The man who tries methods, ignoring principles, is sure to have trouble." It's pretty easy to see that if you're experiencing trouble, you're focusing on the wrong thing. There is no scarcity of methods and tactics, tricks and

tips, fads and fashions in the sales business. But ignoring the principles and continuing to experiment with one method after another will not lead to success. Instead, it's a recipe for trouble.

Studying and learning methods alone will not reveal why something works or doesn't work. Studying principles and how to apply them allows you to create your own methods. Any method of selling will work, as long as it aligns with the fundamental principles underlying all sales activities.

The ingredients for success in any area of life or living are simple:

a) *Know the principles.*

b) *Develop methods that work.*

NEVER COMPLAIN – NEVER EXPLAIN

Losers are always *complaining and explaining,* looking for reasons and justifications why their sales are in a slump. And they seem to take a perverted pleasure out of being critical, censorious, condemning or contemptuous of those who are trying to get the job done. In my opinion, it's not only offensive, it is just plain lazy.

On the other hand, a winner never complains and never explains. They face the problem, make a clear assessment of the situation, and *get something done.*

Instead of looking at what is really going on and what needs to be done, a loser frantically searches for something to explain his failures.

In business - when times are tough - you'll always hear complaints like this: "*The economy is slow; things are tight all over; nobody's buying anything these days.*"

The list of explanations is as endless as it is useless because excuses are often just a way of letting you off the hook for giving up. If all you're looking for is an excuse, you can always find one. But if you really want something done, you can find a way. It all depends on your point of view.

And you'll have lots of people agreeing with you, as misery does love company, doesn't it?

For example, several years ago the owner of a company where sales were seriously down called me in for a consultation and evaluation. I met with the President (not the owner) of the company. I found that he had adopted a *very convincing* explanation (meaning a way of avoiding the problem) of why sales were slow. He had been spending all his time searching through newspapers, magazines, and other media to explain the problem and doing nothing to actually find a solution.

His focus was so fixed on blaming others and looking for reasons *to explain his failure*, that he was blind to the real source of the problem.

So, I decided to let him tell me all about it, and to try to *convince me* why his sales were down and that nothing could be done. This opened Pandora's box, literally.

Like a fire hose, all the garbage (opinions, explanations and wrong assumptions) he had collected to convince himself that nothing could be done, came rushing out in a torrent.

When he finally wound down, he paused, looked at me hopelessly, and waited for some indication of my agreement, asking, "So, what do you think?"

I reflected for a moment before I said, solemnly,

"You're right, it does sound hopeless. But, if everything you've said here is true, we've got nothing to talk about. I'm sorry, but I can't help you."

As I got up to leave, he cried out, *"Hey, where are you going? Can't you see I'm dying here? I need help."*

I sat back down, saying, "*Well okay then, now we've got something to talk about.*"

This was the turning point. At least now we had a chance, as he wasn't incapable, just misdirected.

He had what I call *a whack on the side of the head.* He realized that he was being part of the problem instead of looking for a solution.

Simply put, once he stopped focusing on *complaining and explaining* and started *doing,* we were able to get him going on a program that would handle what needed to be done.

Once he got out-of-the-way of himself and back into action, everything came together. All the usual business solutions and promotional actions started to get some traction. That simple shift of attention made all the difference.

He realized that if he were looking only for *failure support*, he would find it. But nothing else would get done. However, if he was looking for *success possibilities*, they *could,* and *would* be found. And then he'd get something done that needed doing, now.

The stock in trade of losers is explanations, justifications and complaints and they're good at what they do; they never run out of excuses.

Like the old Yiddish proverb says,

Law: "If you don't want to do something, one excuse is as good as another."

Winners ignore the infinity of reasons why something can't be done. Instead they focus on one thing: getting it done in spite of every invitation to do otherwise.

NON-VERBAL CLUES

It's said that body language and tone of voice make up 90% of communication; words only about 10 percent.

If this is true, doesn't it make sense that we should know a lot more about body language?

Dale Carnegie gives his opinion on the subject:

"We are evaluated and classified by these four contacts: *what we do, how we look, what we say, and how we say it.*"

In my experience, people believe *non-verbal* over verbal clues; preferring to believe *what they see over what they hear.* They instinctively look for and trust *what you're not saying* that will enable them to find out more about you.

They do this by picking up *non-verbal clues* that can work for or against you. Rest (un) assured, that in spite of the sincerity and conviction of your words, if you leave just a *1% thread of doubt* in their minds, you can forget the deal.

It is axiomatic that the worst thing you can do is to create doubt in a prospect or customer. And the more you talk, the more you increase the chances to screw up.

Overselling, as we know, can be a fatal and expensive mistake. Avoid this pitfall by being *totally consistent* in every detail of the message you're trying to get across. This means, say exactly what you want to say, and *nothing else.*

Selling is a craft that requires discipline, direction and discretion over what you say and how you say it. It's not random chitchat about meaningless subjects. It is *communication with a purpose.* And everything you do or say either does meaningful work to forward that purpose or it hinders it.

Some examples of non-verbal clues are: When you answer the phone, is your tone of voice consistent with a welcoming, interested attitude? Does your voice itself convey a smile?

How do you treat employees or waitresses?

Do you return phone calls as expected, or invent reasons why you didn't.

Do you show up when promised or invent some lame excuse why you were late?

Do you follow through with a promised favor, or offer a rationalization instead?

All of these clues and more convey a *non-verbal message* of *who you really are.* You must be *consistent* - and this means *all the time.*

Everything about you must be *doing something worthwhile* in getting your message across. *Inconsistency* in your message can create doubt, which can stop your sale in an instant.

Here are some tips to remember:

Evaluate your sales presentation regularly or have someone else do it for you.

Ruthlessly eliminate all the weak points that don't contribute to your message.

Get rid of the baggage and unnecessary clutter that can creep into your presentation and clean house of all your verbal and non-verbal elements.

Here is the fundamental principle behind this:

Law: People can believe your words and *still doubt your message.*

Be honest and consistent in every aspect of your verbal and non-verbal interactions with your clients and you'll avoid this potentially fatal flaw in your sales presentations.

Above all, *don't give them a reason to doubt you.*

Law: Inconsistency generates doubt. Doubt equals indecision. Indecision means no sale.

And finally, once again, Ralph Waldo Emerson does not disappoint:

"When the eyes say one thing, and the tongue another, a practiced man relies on the language of the first."

Chapter 6

ON BEING HUMAN

Yes, we all belong to a species of humans called *Homo sapiens,* Latin for *wise human* or *knowing human*; no big surprise here. Even the distinguishing characteristics of *being human*: the ability to act with intelligence, judgment and to use communication for self-expression and the exchange of ideas are pretty well known and agreed upon.

But nowhere is it claimed that human beings are perfect. Rather, the implication is that *being human* is equivalent to being capable of making mistakes.

While it is said that perfection exists in the *minds-eye only,* far too many give themselves a life sentence inside *the prison of perfection*, by demanding only perfection and accepting nothing less. It's a trap.

You must not let the *obsession for perfection* suffocate your creativity. Instead, be yourself and strive to do the best you can with the cards you're dealt.

Albert Einstein evidently agrees: "*We have to do the best we can. This is our sacred human responsibility.*"

Freedom from this *trap* is possible, once you recognize that you too, are *human*.

And there is no such thing as a perfect human being; mistakes come with the territory; absolute perfection is unattainable on this planet and arguably, any other.

Instead, seek to make steady progress toward your goals, adjusting and improving as you go, striving to become better than you were yesterday.

This is a worthy goal and one to which many others agree:

"Perfection is not attainable, but if we chance perfection we can catch excellence." – Vince Lombardi

"The man with insight enough to admit his limitations comes nearest to perfection." – Johann Wolfgang von Goethe

"Practice is a means of inviting the perfection desired." – Martha Graham

Instead of being satisfied with nothing less than perfection, a commendable goal might instead be to become a shining example of *being human in an imperfect world,* at least in my opinion . . . of course, being imperfect, I could be wrong (smile).

OPEN BEFORE YOU CLOSE

Before you can ever hope to close a deal, you have to make a connection and *open a relationship* with an individual customer or prospect.

And that process takes as long as it takes, you can't rush it and you can't skip it if you hope to close a deal.

Here are five tips; each one a natural law:

1. Get on the same page as the person you're talking to. *Find things you have in common.*

2. *Tell a story they can relate to.* Facts and figures only make people think, not act.

3. *Be interested in them* more than you are yourself.

4. Don't start talking before they're ready to start listening - stop talking *before* they stop listening.

5. Don't rush or force. Avoid creating *sales resistance* that wasn't there to begin with.

Open a relationship first and at least you'll have a chance to close a deal. Fail to open a relationship first and you'll never seal the deal.

OPEN "SESAME"

Has anyone ever casually asked you this question? *"So, what business are you in?"*

Did your answer create confidence and opportunity or negate it?

Every successful salesperson must know the secret to answering this question effectively – and now so will you. First your answer has to accomplish one thing: It must attract their attention. If what you say is also able to spur their curiosity, this magically becomes the *open sesame* to further engaging their interest in you.

The back-story on the phrase *open sesame* comes from an Arabic adventure tale titled, *Ali Baba and the Forty Thieves*.

As the story goes, Ali Baba overheard a group of 40 thieves reveal two magic words, which when spoken, would allow entrance to their treasure trove of gold. The two secret words were *open sesame*. And once Ali Baba knew the secret, he used it to open the door to the trove and gather the gold for himself.

Similarly, there are two *magic words* in all sales success.

They are: *attention and curiosity*.

If you can attract attention and spark curiosity you will have entered on the first step to a possibility of a sale.

First, what is attention?

It is a directed or focused awareness on something or someone. People tend to create what they put their attention on, so if you can attract someone's attention, they naturally become interested or curious about you.

Now, as there are always different stimuli, external and internal vying for their attention, you have to be able to rise above those things and engage their attentiveness more than the others.

How do you do this? It's easy to figure out. Just ask yourself, "What gets your attention?" Isn't it usually something you didn't expect, a surprise, a challenge, a question, or a different way of saying something that captures your attention and stimulates your thoughts?

And what is curiosity? It is a desire to learn or know more. It is when something surprising, unusual, or novel catches and engages your attention. It comes from the word inquisitive, meaning questioning or interested.

These two words, *attention and curiosity* are essential to any selling activity, without which, no selling will take place.

PERCEPTION AND REALITY

Here is a simple principle of selling that will come in handy once you grasp it.

In any sales activity, *perception, reality, and value* are inextricably intertwined. If you bring about a change in any one point, it will invariably affect the other two. When a client perceives a personal benefit in what you're offering, this becomes more *real and valuable* in their minds.

Law: If they see it, they will believe it. If they believe it, they'll buy it (or want to).

Work out some examples for yourself how these three elements are connected and you will be in for some pleasant surprises.

PERSIST AND PERSEVERE

The first step is easy to take. But what comes next is what separates the winners from losers. The following quote contains the reason why.

"I do not think there is any other quality so essential to success of any kind as the quality of *perseverance*. It overcomes almost everything, even nature."- John D. Rockefeller

Why? Because deeply embedded inside every winner is the determination to *persist and persevere* in spite of impossible odds.

Persistence is omnipotent, but at the same time, you always run into those people that tell you that you're being too pushy. In their minds, if you're the *least bit* assertive, you're considered too forceful, aggressive, and too high-pressure.

Such people would prefer that you be politely submissive and never assert your own opinions, or else they think you're considered unpleasant to be around.

While I never recommend arrogant, bullying tactics of overwhelming people, there is a huge difference between being persuasive and being submissive.

The biggest difference is that the overly submissive salesperson will never ask for the order. And, you'll never get the order you don't ask for.

So, yes, it does takes a lot of creative imagination and a bit of audacity in finding new ways of getting your message across without making a pest of yourself. But that goes with the territory of being a professional salesperson, doesn't it?

Question: How do you know when you're going too far?

Answer: Experience tells us that 20% of the time almost any sales effort will meet with success.

So, if you're closing less than 20% of the time, you're being a wimp. And also remember that 60% of all sales are made after the fourth call.

So toughen up your *persistence, perseverance and persuasiveness* and you'll make it onto the winning side of this ledger. I'm not alone in this idea as many of the greatest minds agree:

"Some men give up their designs when they have almost reached the goal; while others, on the contrary, obtain a victory by exerting, at the last moment, more vigorous efforts than ever before."- Herodotus, Greek historian

"The most essential factor is *persistence* – the determination never to allow your energy or enthusiasm to be dampened by the discouragement that must inevitably come." – James Whitcomb Riley.

"A little more persistence, a little more effort, and what seemed hopeless failure may turn to glorious success." - Elbert Hubbard.

"Nothing in the world can take the place of persistence. Talent will not; nothing in the world is more common than unsuccessful men with talent. Genius will not; unrewarded genius is a proverb. Education will not; the world is full of educated derelicts. Persistence and determination alone are omnipotent." – U.S. President Calvin Coolidge

The route to distinction in the sales profession begins in your *will to prevail* and succeeds by persistence, perseverance and persuasiveness.

PERSONAL INITIATIVE IN *ACTION*

For any salesperson, it all starts with one indispensable requisite for success: personal initiative.

So, what is it? *Initiative* means to start or cause a motion to begin *without being ordered* or forced to do so. It's the ability to act on your own and make decisions without the help or advice from others.

Those who possess this quality of initiative do not stand about idly waiting to be ordered to do things; they simply get busy getting things done. The impetus does not stem from externally generated coercion or force, nor is it required, as initiative stems unbidden from within.

In everyday language, *personal initiative in action* means, *you see what needs to be done, and do it (without being told).*

In 1899, Elbert Hubbard, wrote a wildly popular book on the subject of personal initiative in action; it was titled, *A Message To Garcia,* and sold over forty million copies and was translated into 37 languages.

It is a story about *initiative* - doing what had to be done without questioning how to do it – or looking for an excuse why it couldn't be done. This is his essay on the subject of initiative in action.

INITIATIVE

THE WORLD BESTOWS ITS BIG PRIZES, both in money and honors, for but one thing. And that is Initiative.

What is Initiative? I'll tell you: It is doing the right thing without being told.

But next to doing the thing without being told is to do it when you are told once. That is to say, carry the Message to Garcia: those who can carry a message get high honors, but their pay is not always in proportion.

Next, there are those who never do a thing until they are told twice: such get no honors and small pay.

Next, there are those who do the right thing only when Necessity kicks them from behind, and these get indifference instead of honors, and a pittance for pay. This kind spends most of its time polishing a bench with a hard-luck story.

Then, still lower down in the scale than this, we have the fellow who will not do the right thing even when some one goes along to show him how and stays to see that he does it: he is always out of a job, and receives the contempt he deserves, unless he happens to have a rich Pa, in which case

Destiny patiently awaits around the corner with a stuffed club. To which class do you belong?

LISTEN TO WHAT THEY'RE *NOT SAYING*

It's a well-known fact that most salespeople keep on talking long after the customer has quit listening. But others from many varied professions share the same sentiment.

Hakan Hardenberger, International Trumpet Master agrees when he says, "Most people don't listen. Real listening means to listen before you play."

And from Ernest Hemmingway, "When people talk, listen completely. Most people never listen."

And from Bernard M. Baruch, American financier, philanthropist, and statesman, "Most of the successful people I've known are the ones who do more listening than talking."

"When we fear what other people think about us, we are frequently more focused on 'being interesting' and less focused on 'taking an interest.' That's why many people talk a great deal when they are anxious and why many people never feel heard. If both people and conversation are trying to be interesting, there is no one left to genuinely listen." – John Yokoyama, owner of the world-famous Pike Place Fish Market in Seattle.

To the professional salesperson, all this simply translates to: Listen as much as you talk.

Maybe it's because most sales reps know too much about what they're selling. Maybe they're so impressed with the dulcet tones of their own voices that they think everyone else will be. Or maybe they're just nervous and can't tolerate the silence. Whatever the reason, just because you know everything about your company and its products and services, doesn't mean that you have to exhaustively tell the customer all that you know. Sure, you have to talk. And you should know more than your customers about what you're selling.

But they don't need to hear everything you know to be in a state of mind to buy what you're selling. So, what is the balance between technical information and simple basic concepts?

It's the precise ratio between technical information and simple basics necessary to *get your message across*.

Just tell them what they want to know and need to hear. And if you're doing all the talking, you'll never even find out what they're looking for. Why? It's simple. You didn't let them tell you. Stop talking so much and start listening more. And I don't mean, *passive listening* where you're only vaguely hearing them talk while planning your next sentence.

I mean, *active listening* - where all your attention is on what they are saying so you can pick up on the subtle nuances that would otherwise be missed. Basically they are telling you how they want to be sold, but you'll only find this out by carefully listening to them.

It's as simple as that. Any further complication is unnecessary. Just start listening more and talking less and you'll discover how you can help them.

Finally, to wrap it up, this quote from Peter Drucker, Austrian-born American management consultant, educator, and author,

"The most important thing in communication is to hear what isn't being said."

PLAY TO YOUR STRENGTHS

On of the best pieces of advice I can give to any aspiring salesperson is to *play to your strengths*, an idea supported by many others:

"Concentrate on your strengths, instead of your weaknesses; on your powers, instead of your problems." – Paul J. Meyer

The power of using this simple concept cannot be overstated. Many advise you to do exactly the opposite, as in, *no pain - no gain*. Apparently, they think you should focus *only* on improving your weaknesses.

Of course, learning to use new tools is necessary and desirable at times, but as a steady diet, your morale will begin to suffer if you don't at least put some balance into the picture and focus on your strengths. Successful people aren't necessarily great at everything.

They recognize their natural, native gifts and strengthen them. By focusing on areas that are easy and interesting they quickly rise to the top in their areas of activity.

Everyone has a natural aptitude for something. Don't feel that you have to be a generalist and do everything. Focus on what you like and are good at naturally, then expand on that.

You really are *one of a kind*, and this is often the sole distinguishing factor that separates you from the din of other salespeople vying for the attention of the buying public.

Confident people don't concentrate on their weaknesses; they focus on refining and strengthening their natural abilities while steadily improving their weak spots.

Areas that you tend to avoid such as cold calling, handling objections, closing techniques or public speaking etc. should be worked on for sure, but not when you're in front of the client.

Pick your battles and choose the time to fight them and you'll improve your game generally without compromising what you're already doing well.

Law: What you focus on tends to show up.

WHAT DO PEOPLE BUY AND *WHY* DO THEY BUY IT?

These are age-old questions (what and why people buy anything) that many have struggled with, but no one seems to have stated the simple answer that can be used in selling.

Surveys don't provide the complete answer, neither do academic studies based on colors, shapes or designs or complex psychological research on the hierarchy of needs. All the assumptions, speculations, and hypothetical theories - developed for the sake of argument - fail to provide something that can make the job of selling easier and more effective.

So, as this book is for use by professional salesmen and women, not just for publication in an academic journal somewhere that is never read or used, we're looking for a workable answer that can be instantly put to use, today, aren't we? My opinion is that the simple (and workable) answer to the questions posed in the title is this:

Law: People are naturally motivated to secure what they need and what they want to survive.

You are not selling a product as much as you are satisfying an instinctive urge. The product is only a physical representation of an invisible impulse.

If you think you are selling only a refrigerator a new dress, a cordless drill, a house painting, a haircut or a pulled tooth, you're missing the boat. And as any good marksman will tell you, if you're aiming at the wrong target, you won't hit the bull's eye. The real pros, the ones who seem to have that *magic touch,* use a bit of knowledge that you need to know to sell to your full ability.

A fundamental principle of sales is subtly at work in every sale you make:

Law: People will be interested in buying only when they see a potential benefit or solution in what you're selling.

People since time immemorial have had troubles in life with all manner of people and things, much the same as today. Their worries or stresses are not always visible, but they exist nonetheless as they are emotional issues and no amount of logic will solve them. If you can discover what they are struggling with, internally or externally, and can also offer them a way out of it, they'll be interested.

As this is, after all, what they need (the logical side) and want (the emotional side). The product or service is secondary to the personal benefit they feel they'll get as a result of the purchase.

This is *what moves them* to buy anything. Although this article is short, it is packed with invaluable information.

Chapter 7

POST-CLOSE CLOSINGS
(First published in Entrepreneur Magazine, 2002)

It's the goal, the purpose, the incentive, the intention, the hope, the dream and the promise of something better. It is the catalyst that stimulates creative thought and drives it into action.

It provides a reason for playing the game. It is, simply, that penultimate moment in the selling process called – *The Close*. It is what all of us are after, whether it be in sales, sports, personal relationships, or any other aspect of life; if you can't close the deal, you won't reap the rewards of your activity.

The Close is where all the preliminary steps in the sales process lead. It is the Emerald City at the end of the Yellow Brick Road, the place where all our efforts culminate in celebratory elation, or come crashing down around us in gloom, disillusionment, and longing for some less volatile, demanding profession.

I'm not adding anything more to what has been written about the techniques of closing the sale in this article. Instead, my focus is to identify and detail the three different stages that occur after you've had that magical moment with the prospect when they have made the decision to go ahead.

The three distinct components to be outlined in this piece are present in almost every modern corporate sale, yet there is almost no mention of them in texts and other articles on the subject. These *Post-Close* Closings cannot be overlooked if one is to achieve long-term success in sales.

To understand, conceptually, what we are looking at, it is necessary to span our attention out a bit beyond just the standard sales close. Before we do step back and look at the procedure from a 30,000-foot viewpoint, lets look more closely at the fundamental elements of a close.

The Close

It is assumed that the reader has at least a rudimentary understanding of the necessary steps leading up to the initial close, and can recognize the closing opportunity when it appears. Nonetheless, a quick review might be of benefit.

First, let's agree upon a simple technical definition for the word *Close*. Paraphrasing liberally from the American Heritage Dictionary, it means, *to bar passage through, to end, to terminate, to enter into an agreement, to bring or come to an appropriate stopping point.*

We shut off the competition; remove the prospect from the presence of other sales people; close the door on them. And pocket the commission. That's what we mean by *The Close*.

But let's not fail to note that it also means to enter into an agreement, and to bring to a conclusion, a stopping point. These concepts are critical to any success in sales.

We could go further and micro-analyze every minute aspect of every small facet of the sales process, like an endless reflection of mirrors, but that would be fruitless.

There is one aspect, however, that bears such scrutiny. It is where an astounding number of otherwise able salespeople botch a perfectly good and simple sale.

The Sales Close

This is a step that should occur the minute you observe that the *Sales Close* has occurred, or in any case, as soon as reasonably possible. It also is the first of what I have termed the *Post-Close Closings*.

The Sales Close is the most familiar and recognizable of the various types of closings. It is simply the final step in a gradient series of steps that are designed to approach the closing in a comfortable manner.

Done correctly, it is as easy as taking the final step up a flight of stairs. It is a win for both buyer and seller, leaving each with the feeling that he has gotten what is needed and wanted from the exchange.

This is where the salesman now has to recognize that he must *Close the Close*. If he doesn't, the sale can slip from his grasp with mercurial and devastating swiftness. He has arrived at the point where the sale can be closed and has succeeded.

That point of awareness has been reached when both parties involved in the sales process are aware of and satisfied with the mutually beneficial agreement that has been reached. The sales closing process should be ended at that point.

To push it further, and continue any purely selling activity beyond this point, the salesperson runs the risk of alienating the prospect. The prospect will tend to put up resistance where before none existed. The salesman can unwittingly create doubt where previously there was certainty.

The prospect will begin to question aspects of the product or service with which he had no problem earlier.

This, in turn, leads the salesperson (erroneously) to believe that he must continue the selling process.

Unfortunately, this leads to an even worse dilemma. The prospect begins trying to stop the salesperson from doing more selling, and the salesman, sensing the withdrawal, starts to dig in and sell even harder.

Thus, the more he pushes, the farther away the prospect retreats, initiating a vicious circle.

Sometimes a botched *Sales Close* can be repaired by directing the prospect's attention back to the earlier point when he was first sold, thereby rehabilitating the comfortable atmosphere and feeling of commitment that existed at that time.

But the best solution by far, is just not to have made this error in the first place. It is far easier to observe, recognize, and acknowledge the characteristics in the prospect that signal that he now understands what is being sold and has become enlightened as to how it can benefit him or his interests and is prepared to move forward. At that point, the selling procedure should come to an end. You have achieved your *Sales Close*, and now you should conclude it.

So, the proper procedure for closing the *Sales Close* is simply this:

1. *Observe* that a close is possible.

2. *Recognize* when a close has actually occurred.

3. *Acknowledge* that this close is the end of any purely selling activity, and that to continue trying to sell past this point could compromise the whole process.

Now, if only that were the end of the overall process we could just leave and collect our commissions. But, alas, there are two more *Post-Close Closes* that must be achieved.

This sometimes dreaded step involves activities of other individuals, behind closed doors, looking over the legal and contractual aspects of your sales close. These are mostly professionals who are dedicated to and paid for finding what is wrong with this contract, often to your detriment. You will rarely, if ever, get to talk to them directly, and they are not there to be sold, in any case. But, as this step is inevitable in corporate selling of any size, it is better to accept that it will occur, and work through it as swiftly and effectively as possible.

Most often, it is best to have your legal department deal with the client's attorneys on contractual language. This is due to what is commonly referred to as *the lawyer-to-lawyer communication rule.*

That is, from a lawyer's point of view, they can always communicate better with other lawyers. Whatever the reason, this rule seems to exist, so we might as well use this knowledge to our advantage to get the job done.

A definition of the *Legal Close* is offered here for descriptive purposes.

The Legal Close
Actions taken by legal professionals that result in a legally binding, written contractual agreement representing the mutual understanding and satisfaction between both parties, completed in a timely manner.

The legal close is important and not to be taken lightly. The overall sale can be lost at this point due to various elements. It is sometimes used to grind down either the price or the terms to a more favorable level.

Taken too far, this grinding can disfigure the agreement you worked so hard to reach earlier, to the point that it is no longer viable or even recognizable.

But hopefully, through vigilance, skillful communication, and persistence, you will prevail in the manner desired. It should not go unnoticed, however, as in the previous step that you have to observe, recognize, and acknowledge the completion of this step.

The contractual elements must be handled conclusively. Sometimes they will accept your contract as is, but usually they will draft one that their lawyers are familiar with and incorporate the elements necessary.

In any case, this is a legal close and should be ended when the mutual agreement is finally contained in the contract, and is legally binding on both parties.

Unfortunately, it's not yet time to celebrate, for there is another danger-ous foe equally capable of scuttling your commission. The administrators wait.

The Administrative Close

When all necessary paperwork is fully completed and in the hands of the proper personnel, the transfer of funds for product or service can and usually does take place.

Though perhaps a bit dull and mundane when compared to the emo-tional high derived from pulling off an important sales close, it is crucial that this step be fully concluded. Once again, it can't be stated too often that it is the *salesman that drives this process.*

It is his responsibility to make sure this *administrative close* actually takes place, even though others may actually be doing the work. The job can-not be considered fully complete until this is done. Once it is introduced into the "machinery" of the business and begins to operate without con-stant further attention, the salesman can consider this step complete, not before.

The Final Act

In common language, this means, *it ain't over 'til it's over.* And that means utterly done. In regard to this, the final act, the salesman has to function as an *executive.*

For a working definition of executive, lets take a look at the derivation of the word, which is: *to execute, to carry out fully, to put completely into effect and to do what is called for.*

It can easily be seen then, that an executive is the one who *gets something done.*

The *salesman as executive* has to monitor the overall sale with great atten-tion to fine detail so that each step is fully completed before moving to the next. The sales executive must have the sales process, the successful methods and procedures for his particular product or service down cold. Any weakness in his knowledge of this process will be exposed instantly under the pressure of an actual selling activity.

He or she should face and handle any deficiency he knows to exist before it becomes embarrassingly apparent to everyone when revealed in front of the client. But this is just the beginning.

Any professional sales executive also must be ready to take complete responsibility for seeing that the sale is brought to a successful conclusion after that first Sales Close. And that takes at least three separate closes:

1. The Sales Close
2. The Legal Close
3. The Administrative Close

His own personal prosperity and the ultimate success of the business depend upon what he does regarding these actions above.

Fail to do them, and we all have to work harder for less. Do them, and we'll all win.

Note: First published in 2002 in Entrepreneur.com magazine under the nom de plume, Jacob Wright.

QUICK THINKING, FAST ACTION

Long-term survival in the sales business depends on your ability to *think quickly and act faster* than your competition.

The following story illustrates this point.

As it goes, a tough chairman of a major company on Wall Street stopped into a well known restaurant simply named '21' for a quick bite.

Not being very hungry he asked the waiter for half of a sirloin steak. Normally the waiter would simply have told him the restaurant didn't serve half-steaks, but given the importance of this customer the waiter agreed and left for the kitchen.

Unbeknownst to the waiter, the chairman followed him to the kitchen to tell him he wanted the steak rare. As the waiter announced to the chef, "*I need a half-steak for a real jerk,*" he also noticed the chairman standing behind him.

Without missing a stroke, the waiter continued to comment to the chef, *and the other half goes to this gentleman.*

This demonstrates the **quick thinking and fast action** on the part of the waiter, narrowly avoiding a very embarrassing situation.

There are three elements that comprise the underlying principle at work in this story:

1. A keen ability to *see* a real or potential threat of danger, before it happens.
2. The willingness and imagination to assess and *decide* upon the correct action to take
3. The courage to *respond* instantly without hesitation or doubt, once the right choice has been made.

The ability to correctly *observe* incipient danger is a result of training, experience and familiarity with the area under investigation.

The willingness to decide stems from the ability to evaluate what's important and what's not, and to think logically.

To respond with *swift, effective action* is a direct result of trusting in your *response-ability* for your actions.

Quick thinking and fast action will help you avoid more trouble than you imagine.

SALES QUOTES TO LIVE BY

Inspiration comes from many sources. Here are a few of my favorite one-liners that I've found valuable over the years.

ZIG ZIGLAR: Your attitude, not your aptitude, will determine your *altitude.*

TOM HOPKINS: You are your greatest asset. Put your time, effort and money into training, grooming, and encouraging your greatest asset.

JEFFREY GITOMER: Obstacles can't stop you. Problems can't stop you. Most of all, other people can't stop you. *Only you* can stop you.

DALE CARNIEGE: 15% of business success comes from professional ability, the rest from your ability to express ideas and to arouse enthusiasm.

ELBERT HUBBARD: To avoid criticism, do nothing, say nothing, be nothing.

JACK CANFIELD: In sales there are usually four or five "no's" to get one yes.

JOE GIRARD: The elevator to Health, Happiness & Success is out of order – you'll have to use the stairs – *one step at a time.*

OG MANDINO: Always render more and *better service than is expected* of you, no matter what your task may be.

JOHN C. MAXWELL: It's difficult to find common ground when all you're focused on is *yourself.*

JIM ROHN: If you really want to do something, you'll find a way. If you don't, you'll find and excuse.

DANIEL JACOBS: All selling boils down to contacting *people* and selling to an *individual.*

STEPHEY R. COVEY: *First understand, then be understood.*

WARNING ABOUT MONEY ISSUES

A merica humorist and writer, Mark Twain stated,

"It ain't what you don't know that gets you into trouble. It's what you know for sure that just ain't so."

Applying this concept to the sales close is also why you should not believe every thought that comes to your mind; because they *'just might be untrue.*

If you regularly have problems asking for money at the close of a deal, the problem is not with the customer. *You are the problem.*

For example, if you have personal thoughts about money being too scarce, or that money is the root of evil, or the old saying that *behind big money is big crime,* or any other thoughts like these, I guarantee that you are losing sales because of it.

You had better handle your own considerations on money, fast!

Thinking about money or how much you're going to make when the deal closes is one of the worst things you can do when you're trying to close a deal.

As I mentioned earlier in this book, *attention tends to follow attention.* When you're thinking about money, the customer will be too. And this is not what you want their attention on.

You want it on the benefits they will enjoy as a result of making the purchase or signing the contract. This is also precisely where your attention must be also, if you hope to close the deal.

Thinking about money is fine, but at the right place and the right time. Money should come to your attention *after you've closed the deal, not before and not during.*

The lyrics from the chorus of the hit song "The Gambler" by Kenny Rogers come to mind:

"You never count your money, when you're sitting at the table; there'll be time enough for counting, *when the dealing's done."*

Get all this straightened out in your mind *before* you start to close the deal and you'll save yourself a lot of trouble.

SALES LONGEVITY

Sales longevity is not just measured by the length of time at the job, but also the value you give others through your efforts, as *giving value to others* is the one of the keys to happiness and a long career.

The word longevity stems from Latin, longaevus, meaning, *long-lived*; something all of us wish for especially in the profession of sales. Here are twelve points for success, which also happen to be basic principles with *universal applicability.*

1. Be true to yourself.

2. Be worthy of trust and give value to others.

3. Be sincerely interested in people.

4. Ensure that people are the most important part of every sale.

5. Take care of people first and the business second.

6. Keep it simple. Keep it real. Be yourself.

7. Under-promise and over-deliver.

8. Never force the customer.

9. Find a way get what *they want and need* as painlessly as possible.

10. Never forget that selling is a human activity of exchange *for mutual benefit.*

11. Market to people, sell to *the individual.*

12. How you make them feel creates an indelible impression forever etched into their memory.

SALES MATURITY

This subject, in my opinion, has received insufficient attention in most books on selling. But there is something you need to know to guarantee long-term survival in the profession.

It is well known among the initiated that selling can often be a very stressful profession. Frustration and rejection come with the territory. There may be times in your life when you feel angry, hopeless, even apathetic and ready to throw in the towel and find an easier profession.

Luckily, it's not always that way. But if you expect long-term survival in selling, you must learn to face and conquer at least two important things.

First, you must learn to *master your emotions.* In fact, succumbing to irrational emotional responses while selling is one of the *most important personal barriers you have to overcome.*

Why? Because your emotions can work for you or against you.

All your *emotional reactions* stem from you and can cause you to act or react in undesirable ways. Although discussed earlier, here is a review of the subject.

Review: The word *emotion* comes from the Old French word *esmovoir,* which means to excite; and the Latin word *movere,* which means *to move.*

When your emotions are triggered, the natural inclination is to instantly respond excitedly, often bypassing logical thought.

But whatever the external stimuli, the fact remains that ultimately you choose how to react or not. And the best path is to act on principle rather than the emotion of the immediate situation.

Emotional reactions tend *to cloud reason* and rationality, keeping you from observing a situation clearly. And you can end up missing opportunities that you should have seen.

Anger, expressed or suppressed, can also be one of the most destructive emotions when out of control. It can blind you to things that you must be aware of to make rational choices, (phrases like *blind with anger, or blind rage* come to mind). It is also obvious to everyone that *you have lost control* of the situation.

At this point the tendency to resort to forcing the customer, client, or prospect comes to the fore, which invariably creates that dreaded enemy of closing a sale: *sales resistance.* Nothing creates tension and stress faster than anger in a sales situation. It creates doubt and distrust, which in turn foster indecision, which is guaranteed to squelch a sale faster than the Christmas spirit in January.

Impatience, second only to anger as a destructive emotional response, is also a major impediment to sales success making you appear immature, weak, and inexperienced.

Mastery of your emotions combined with a healthy dose of patience (and persistence) will guard you from making major errors and missing big opportunities.

I admit these things don't come naturally. It takes focused, disciplined practice to conquer ingrown habits of acting only on emotion instead of logic.

Sales maturity develops as a direct consequence of the practiced ability to respond appropriately as a professional with your attention on the big picture, instead of with the immature, emotional overreaction of an amateur. In dealing with people and interpersonal relationships, especially

- in business situations when customers are under the stress of spending money and their commitment – these are key skills you must develop if you hope to attain and remain successful.

Remaining interested in the client (no matter what the provocation to do otherwise); keeping your *attention on their feelings* (while keeping your emotions under control); and maintaining a focus on *adding value* can foster an atmosphere of professionalism and *sales maturity* to the equation that can put you into the big leagues!

SALES SKILLS TUNE-UP

Let's assume you're awake, walking and talking, but you know *you're not quite on your game.* We've all felt this way at times; you just need a little something to get you at your peak right out the chute.

Any professional athlete feels the same. Their warm-up may take ten minutes or an hour, but they are acutely aware that their success is on the line every time the game starts. The game of *selling is no different.*

So, how much warm-up is enough?

Those experienced in such things have said that if you spend too much time warming up, you'll miss the race, but fail to warm up at all and you may not finish the race. I agree.

In selling, the purpose of a warm-up is to clear your mind and sharpen your focus on your tools and on the customer. It doesn't have to be an overhaul every time you warm-up, just a fast tune-up.

The following points should give you all you need to jump-start your day and get in shape to make the most of every opportunity.

Begin by reading the following points - *each one is a natural law of selling* - for 10 minutes at the beginning of your day. Then set aside one minute to look them over as a quick reminder just before your sales presentation. I think you'll notice some fast, dramatic improvements.

1. *Just Show up.* It's the first rule of selling. All other steps in the sales process hinge on this first one.

2. *Capture Attention and Excite Imagination.* Show them something new that will get them curious about the future, something more than they expected.

3. *Don't Assume Anything.* You're always better off to assume you *know nothing about the clients needs.* This forces you to *listen, learn and lead.*

4. *Find their pain.* Basically, you're *selling hope* that something can be done about their troubles. Many have given up on the fact that anything can be done at all (about what they're struggling with). Tell a story that gives them hope. Let them know they're not alone. Then show them how others have been helped with what you're offering.

5. *Objections are closing opportunities.* Many times, objections are red herrings and not really the problem. Don't take the bait. Observe carefully, remain interested, and handle with finesse.

   Find out how important the objection is to them. Is it a deal-killer, or an incidental? Ask, "What would you like me to do about that?" Often it's something that can be handled easily. Then ask, "If I can get that (the objection) handled, are you prepared to move ahead with the proposal?"

6. *Logic makes people think, emotion makes people act.* Remember that *emotion is the secret weapon* that all successful sales people use. The most effective way of engaging them emotionally is to *tell a story they can relate to.*

7. *Close one step at a time.* You only run into *sales resistance* when you skip a step in the sales process. When you see this happening, go back to when they were doing well, and find out what they didn't understand or what they disagreed with. Handle it and come forward. It's like walking up a set of stairs. The final step (the close) is easy to take if you've comfortably taken each step before it.

8. *People only buy a benefit.* If they don't see it and feel something that will benefit their own self-interest, all manner of difficulties will develop.

The light bulb of recognition will be evident when they see the benefit for themselves. When you see that, simply close the deal with, "Let's get you started so you can get the results you've hoped for."

9. *Know when to stop selling.* When the sale is closed, *stop selling.* This is the most common mistake salespeople make. Any further selling after this point has been reached will backfire on you and build up resistance that *wasn't there to begin with.*

10. *Handle the paperwork.* Many sales are lost because of poor handling of the paperwork. *Be prepared.*

Have all your paperwork with you and within arms length. Know exactly where it is and how to execute a contract. Even if it's just a preliminary agreement, *get something in writing.*

Review each of the 10 points before your next appointment and see what happens. I think you'll be happily surprised at the results.

SALES SUCCESS TRIANGLE

Professional musicians, those in the top 2% of their field, have internalized these three factors until they have become a way of life:

(1) *Practice* - done alone; to focus on the rough spots and perfect technique.

(2) *Rehearse* - done with a group, to use what they have practiced in cooperation with others.

(3) *Perform* - solely for the audience. The intention is only to *contact, connect and convey* their musical message to the public. If they haven't practiced for perfection, and rehearsed for coordination and confidence,

weaknesses show up in the rehearsal and the performance will definitely suffer.

The same is true in selling.

To reach the top in the sales profession, you have to do three things very well. These three elements are called the *Sales Success Triangle.*

It is made up of three corners, each of equal importance:

1. Practice
2. Drilling
3. Presentation

Practice and individual study is done alone until perfected.

Drilling and group training is done by interaction with others to work out the bugs and get used to handling yourself under pressure. Presentation is focused on the clients or customers.

Practice – Practice in selling means to *prepare* by repeatedly going over your presentation by yourself, again and again, and not just working on what you already do well, but working on your rough spots until perfected.

I have found this quote to be a welcome reminder from Sir William Osler, The Father of Modern Medicine:

"By practice alone you can become expert."

Need to increase your confidence? The key is found in focused, disciplined practice. Then practice more and more again. Ideally, to get your presentation down perfectly, you have to do it at least 1,000 times - and do it correctly until it becomes part of your DNA, totally your own, natural and effortless.

And if you need further motivation to practice, here is something from Arnold Palmer, world famous golf immortal and highly successful business executive.

"It's a funny thing, the more I practice, the luckier I get."

Drilling – Sales training or drilling is like rehearsing for a performance.

Go over your presentation with one or several others where you're exposed to pressures that you don't have with practicing alone. Learn to act and react to unexpected situations presented by the people you're drilling with so that you maintain a calm, effortless professionalism at all times.

Rehearsals provide a life-like situation, but with a chance to stop and work on anything that needs work or correction, so you can get your skills up to professional standards.

Sales training, drilling and rehearsing will *expose the weak spots* that you need to work on. Welcome them, because, if you don't smooth them out now, they will eventually show up in front of the client, and usually at the most inopportune moment.

Remember that every time you get better at something, you also learn a way to make it even better.

Any time you run into a seemingly insurmountable challenge (and you will run into them), remember this quote:

"The best way out is always through." - Robert Frost

Presentation – This is the real deal. You're on your own in front of the public. It's easy if you've done your homework with individual practice and group rehearsals. This is how you work your way up to true professional competence.

You will see your weak points and your strengths instantly as the client, prospect or group you're talking to will let you know when you're off the mark.

The seasoned veteran professional has done this over 10,000 times. Confidence in your presentation is built on drilling it to perfection - and that comes from practice! My personal experience shows that the drilling to presentation ratio is about 60:1. This breaks down to one hour of preparation for each minute of presentation time. And in my experience, this is true!

Yes, this adds up to 60 hours of your disciplined attention to perfection in drilling your skills in communication, handling objections, unexpected situations and more, until they are thoroughly internalized.

Of course, once you have your basic fundamentals down cold, it takes far less time to give yourself a "tune-up" to be at the top of your game.

Your presentation reflects your company and your product or service as much as it does you, alone, for better or worse.

All of your practice and rehearsal training should be so well known that it is second nature by this time. Your attention must be on the audience, not your power point slide show. The presentation is, after all, for the audience (your prospects).

Your focus has to be on *getting your message across* to the people in front of you.

If your practice and preparation were done perfectly, your chances of pulling off a success are very good. Note that any increase or decrease in one of the three corners of the sales success triangle will affect the other two in the same way.

If you increase your practice, your group training exercises will generally improve thus increasing the ease of your performance. More time in front of the public, performing, will show you what you need to practice or drill even more.

This quote by Jim Rohn, American entrepreneur, author and motivational speaker, says it best:

"Take advantage of every opportunity to practice your communication skills so that when important occasions arise, you will have the gift, the style, the sharpness, the clarity, and the emotions to affect other people."

Remember that you are the one in control of the outcome of your presentations and performances. It is the neophyte, the amateur, who blames a failure on his tools, the equipment, the audience, the location or anything else. At the end of the day, you are the main determining factor of the outcome.

Using the sales success triangle will help you take the mystery out of mastering the art of salesmanship. This will enable you to successfully *contact, connect, and convey* your message to your potential customers.

SECRET BASIS OF SUCCESS

"Is there really a *secret basis of success?"* I'm often asked this question and I love to respond – if only because the answer is imbedded in the question. Understanding these three concepts may be enlightening.

Basis is the main component or ingredient, the basic method or system to get something done or organized; the fundamental principle underlying an idea. In plain English, it's the starting point to getting something done.

Success is the attainment of a favorable or desired outcome. Your personal definition of success may differ but the common denominator is still the same. Success is the end product of achieving something you've planned or desired.

The concepts of the words basis and success are mostly well known and familiar to us. But this final element is the *catalyst* that generates the power to get what we desire.

The secret is: *How much do you want it?*

Unless you've got that internal drive supercharging your energy and determination to overcome all obstacles – your plans and intentions for success may fall short.

This mindset is evident in the words of Mary Kay Ash, founder of Mary Kay Cosmetics:

"When you reach an obstacle, turn it into an opportunity. You have the choice. You can overcome and be a winner, or you can allow it to overcome you and be a loser. The choice is yours and yours alone. Refuse to throw in the towel. Go that extra mile that failures refuse to travel. It is far better to be exhausted from success than to be rested from failure."

There are countless examples but they all boil down to one thing: Winners *want it more* than the competition. Nothing is more important.

This *is the secret ingredient* that separates winners from wannabe's. The word, "want" to them, means an intense desire, a strong craving, an almost unquenchable personal *need to be better than they were the day before.*

Think about it. What gets you up in the morning and drives you to keep going all day in spite of everything? What simulates your mind and energizes your body so that you don't even think of obstacles; you just focus on your goal? This is what transforms *dreams into action* – wishes into results – hopes into reality.

One more thing: The sense of doubt or reservation doesn't even enter the equation. It just doesn't exist. This frame of mind is what causes the physical universe to align with your dictates. Honestly ask yourself this question: *How much do I really want it?* Your answer will determine your own *secret basis of success*

Chapter 8

SEEDS OF YOUR FUTURE

This quote by Leonardo da Vinci started me thinking about how present time links the past with the future:

"In rivers, the water that you touch is the last of what has passed and the first of that which comes; so with present time."

It's a well-established fact that what has passed is kept alive and carried forward through memories of what has come before.

If your attention is fixed on past negative emotions of failure, anger, loss, despair, hopelessness, blame, resentment, fear, or regret – these are carried with you into *the present.*

Conversely, if your thoughts are focused on positive feelings of happiness, action, competence, confidence, serenity, forgiveness, friendship, love of life, self and others – these are also carried along with you into *present time.* And, whether positive or negative, the way you look at life, the environment, people and situations in present time, is colored accordingly.

Thereby, *the seeds of your future* are created and carried forward with you at all times; brought into being by your decisions, thoughts, ideas and feelings and kept alive by your continuing attention on them.

As you *tend to create what you keep your attention on*, this can become a prediction of your future.

The future does indeed unfold with inexorable certainty, but in *extremely minute increments*. It doesn't happen all at once.

This is not to say that it takes a long time, it only takes as long as necessary to bring it about. Big changes do occur, but only when preceded by countless small ones. To create a future that you desire, begin right now – in present time.

Start with one *clear, unambiguous decision* of what you intend to accomplish, for at that moment the universe begins a process of aligning to your dictates rather than the reverse, bringing about the changes you desire.

Act in the present as you hope your future to be – and it soon will be.

SELF-DELUSION: THE TRAP

"It is only persistence in *self-delusion and ignorance* which does harm."

These words from Roman Emperor Marcus Aurelius, hit the nail on the head. But then, who among us hasn't downplayed our abilities or engaged in self-criticism or denigration of oneself at one time or another?

While I have no argument with some who consider self-denial an admirable trait, my personal views lie closer to those of Marcus Aurelius.

My opinion is that negation of your knowledge, strength, experience, intelligence and ability is making your life harder than it should be. As the old adage correctly states, *when you doubt your power, you give power to your doubt.*

Life offers plenty of challenge already without knocking yourself down first, especially when trying to carve out a living in the profession of selling. There is no one who has not done things, for which they could be censured, *just don't make a habit of doing such things.*

Recognize your failings and correct them with self-discipline and common sense. There is far, far more good in you than the reverse. Here is a time-honored principle:

Law: Self-doubts and self-confidence alike require constant nurturing and attention to become reality.

So, knock off deliberately weakening and harming yourself, it helps no one but your competition.

DISCIPLINE AND CONTROL

Discipline and control are two sides of the same coin, interdependent, but with each enhancing the other.

Using discipline (willpower over emotion) and control (reason over desire) allows you to choose your own path with confidence and certainty, free from doubt, fear and indecision,

To a salesperson, self-discipline or self-control mean *doing what you've got to do, when you've got to do it.* It means getting the job done no matter what. It means finding a way instead of searching for an excuse.

It means ignoring the useless incessant internal chatter convincing you why something can't be done.

In spite of considerations to the contrary, the terms control and discipline are not natively bad, but sometimes have a negative connotation.

Many equate discipline with punishment, with painful memories of teachers with rulers, tough boot camp sergeants, and other undesirable experiences. Even the word punishment, is one of the definitions for the word discipline. And the word control, often conjures up visions of authority figures forcing you to do something against your will.

Basically though, control means an *orderly, predictable* conduct or pattern of behavior. Nothing wrong with that is there? Perhaps it might be more understandable by comparing it with its opposite - the concept of things being *out of control.*

Instinctively, we know when things are *out of control* – as in a sales cycle for example – it is a clear signal that *something bad is about to happen*. It means things are unmanageable, disorderly, unpredictable and generally undesirable; something to be avoided at all costs.

But if things are *under control*, they are manageable, orderly, predictable and more desirable; and good things are about to happen.

This idea of discipline being positive and predictable control, is something that can benefit people generally and any salesman or woman specifically.

Countless others also support this concept; here are a few examples.

"If we don't discipline ourselves, the world will do it for us." – William Feather

"With self-discipline most anything is possible." – Theodore Roosevelt

"If you're not willing to accept your own discipline, you're not going to accomplish 2% of what you could have." – Tom Hopkins

"Self-discipline is crucial to a simpler, more contented life." – Tenzin Gyatso, the 14th Dalia Lama

"We all have dreams. But in order to make dreams come into reality, it takes an awful lot of determination, dedication, self-discipline, and effort." – Jesse Owens

"Self-respect leads to self-discipline. When you have both firmly under your belt, that's real power." – Clint Eastwood

Discipline and control are not inherently bad, for they open doors of opportunity while preparing you for it at the same time; and put you back in charge of your own life.

CUT YOUR LOSSES

There's an old saying, well known among salespeople that is damnably right:

You can't say the right thing to the wrong person.

Sometimes no matter what you say to the wrong person, it's still wrong. But, almost anything you say to the right person tends to work out.

Let's face facts; you're not going to connect with everyone you meet no matter how hard you try. Under such circumstances, you would be better off finding another person that would be a good fit for them.

Then, you can spend your time and enthusiasm on someone that you'll have at least a chance of success. It's really pretty simple. If you find yourself in a no-win situation, cut your losses and move on.

There is always the chance of another opportunity.

SELLING THE DREAM

Never sell the product – *sell the dream.* This is a familiar concept to top-level poker players when they say, *"Play the man, not the cards."*

Or, the master musician who says, *"don't play the notes, play the music."*

The message is the same, no matter how you say it: **It's always about people** and how you make them feel. You're selling a person on an idea, an opportunity, a lifestyle, a feeling that comes from the dream of **owning** the product, not the product itself. People like to own, they don't like to buy. Owning is fun, sometimes buying isn't but it should be.

For example, even if you're involved in the real estate business, you should be selling the dream, not the product. You're not selling a *house;* you're selling a *home*, an experience, a feeling, an atmosphere and a safe environment.

We live in a new and different world of marketing. The tools at your disposal only 10 years ago are outdated and nearly obsolete.

The Internet is ubiquitous and has taken over. It is, in fact, the greatest direct marketing tool the world has ever seen and it's mostly free, and it's growing exponentially on a daily basis. Use whatever tools are developed and workable, but never forget the one thing that never changes: Sell the dream, not the product.

SALES IS A CONTACT SPORT

You get a little too close to the edge and it hits you – that gripping sensation in the pit of your stomach.

The dizzying feeling of trying to imagine a chasm so immense, that a strange, unexplainable loss of control sweeps over you. Then it hits you.

You're actually looking down at a one-mile deep gorge of the Colorado River. And this is *the real thing!*

A photograph of the Grand Canyon on the other hand – even when expertly done – just doesn't convey the same depth of feeling and sensation. It's better than nothing, but second-hand emotion is never really an acceptable substitute for the real thing, because the *joy of being alive* is a product of actual contact with life.

And the same thing is true in sales.

It's impossible to succeed in sales without actually being in contact with, engaged in, and willing to communicate with people, face to face. No matter how good you are, you simply can't utilize all your skills and talents until you contact and connect with others.

It's not just extreme activities like river rafting, mountain climbing or skydiving that offer this contact or experience. The thrill of being alive and the joy of living are available to you at every moment you're alive, no matter what you're doing.

It all comes down to one thing: The *willingness to experience. This is what it means to be in contact with something or someone.*

If you hate your job, your town or the people in it, then your attention is magnetically attracted to situations and circumstances that reinforce your decision and your unwillingness to experience what is going on around you.

And when you focus only on what you don't want, that is what *you tend to attract.*

On the other hand, if you have the idea that you are *willing to experience* what you are already experiencing, then you'll find that you can survive anything that comes your way.

Knowledge acquired through the senses, rather than some ivory tower abstraction or professorial reasoning, will give you the deep, instinctual and visceral awareness that life is happening for you now! The game of life has started and all that is required is for you to *decide to play* and be *willing to experience* it.

Discard the self-protective ramparts you've constructed and throw yourself into the running stream of life. Embrace friendship and betrayal, beauty and ugliness, success and failure, loss and abundance, hatred and love; they are all part of the *game of life.*

This is how you experience the true joy of living. Once you decide you *are willing to experience it* – everything else is a shabby substitute.

Now, if you're already thinking that this concept *applies directly to sales,* you're right. When it gets down to it, it's not that complicated.

Personal contact is the most effective sales and marketing tool there is. Get into contact with people and then some more people. Keep at it. Be willing to experience whatever comes your way. Persist in spite of everything. Don't shrink back because of minor failures. You'll find that it's not that hard to make a high degree of success in your activities.

Selling really **is** a contact sport; and the ones who win are those who are willing to jump in and experience it.

HANDLING THE INDIVIDUAL

There has never been a successful sale without people being actively involved in the process. But there is something more to it. Selling is indeed about the people generally, but specifically it is about contacting and connecting with an individual customer or prospect:

Law: Sales is about contacting people and selling to the *individual.*

So, get used to it; it's this simple. If you don't find people interesting, if you can't stand listening to them or if you find them irritating, then selling is not for you. It's after all, a prerequisite of the profession.

Everything stems from this: they'll find you interesting when you're interested in them – *as an individual.*

FIRST IMPRESSIONS

An important part of your job is to smooth the edges of the buying process and make it as painless as possible. And making a *favorable first impression* is the first make or break point in the process, well stated by Bruce Burton:

"For good or ill, your conversation is your advertisement. Every time you open your mouth, you let men look into your mind. Do they see it well-clothed, neat, businesswise?" Or otherwise.

Some studies have shown that 55 percent of the first impression you make comes from the visual image, 38 percent from tone of voice, pacing and volume, but only 7 percent from the words you're saying.

Further, you must be aware of how *much time you have* before they decide you are worth listening to: about 2 minutes in face to face, 30 seconds over the phone, and 15 seconds on voicemail.

People also don't like to deal with unfriendly or unpleasant salespeople if they can possibly avoid it and often resent what they have to go through in order to *buy anything.*

If buying has become a pain to them, a necessary evil they have to put up with to get what they want, is it any wonder that Internet sales are growing exponentially? However, this could be the key to opening your sales career that you've been looking for.

Your attitude speaks volumes and happily this is something you can control. The easiest way to change your attitude is to *be interested in them before you meet them.*

Before the appointment, get the idea that your reason for meeting them is to help them get what they need and want, and that nothing is more important. Determine that you are going to find a way to add value to their business and their lives. At the very least, decide that the meeting is going to turn out better than you thought it would.

These things dictate a welcoming attitude that conveys a message before you say a word, often resulting in this attitude being reciprocated by the prospect.

There is a huge window of opportunity left by the *nothing matters* mentality of poor to average salespeople. If you can fill that gap with genuine interest and a sincere, honest, and friendly effort to be helpful, *you'll be in clover.*

One piece of advice: Never feign admiration or interest. Because once they sense it, *and they always do*, you've given them a reason not to do business with you.

This is a great quote to keep in mind while selling:

"You can make more friends in two months by becoming really *interested in other people*, than you can in two years by trying to get other people interested in you." – Bernard Meltzer

SETTING EXPECTATIONS

His statement caught everyone by surprise. *"It's really an expensive suit, it just looks cheap on me,"* he said unashamedly.

We were stunned that a veteran salesman would say that in front of the customer. At first blush it didn't make sense, but as the sales relationship moved forward, it sunk in. He was *setting expectations* that no matter what, he would *tell the truth*. This is a case of handling expectations properly.

As a seasoned salesman, he knew these important things:

1. As much as anything, people base their buying decisions on their *trust in the salesperson first, and the product or the company second.*

2. *Setting expectations* properly is the key to all repeat sales.

3. *Mishandling expectations* is something customers may forgive, but they never forget.

4. *Honesty* really is the best policy.

5. *Expectations imply and create futures.*

Expectations are the anticipation of things that haven't yet occurred and the hope that their trust in you will be rewarded in finding what they really need and want and providing it as promised. Simple forthrightness, truthfulness, common sense, sincerity and integrity will do more to gain their loyalty than anything else you do. They'll buy from you again, when they feel you are honest and are looking out for their best interests *after the sale.*

The best advice I can give you in correctly setting expectations is this: *promise what you can deliver and never promise what you can't deliver.*

If you offer excuses, reasons or justifications instead of predictable results, you have lost a repeat customer for good. No matter what they tell you at the time, they will try to avoid doing business with you again.

When you deliver what you have promised, you have shown that their trust in you was well placed and you have created a potential repeat customer. They'll look for a way to do business with you again. Don't underestimate the value of handling expectations in an honest, realistic way. It is one of the most important ways that you can turn a sale into a satisfied and loyal customer.

GOOD ADVICE

Having these nine ideas under your belt will sometimes dig you out of a hole you didn't know you were in.

1. Nothing can *stop* you unless you first agree that you want to stop.

2. Nothing can *change* you unless you have decided you want to change.

3. Nothing can *start* you until you resolve that you want to start.

4. Nothing can *harm* you unless you first agree that it is harmful.

5. Your life will be as good or bad as you decide it's going to be – a decision no one else can make for you.

6. Need more money? Examine what you can deliver that will add value to others' lives.

7. Your thoughts, decisions, feelings and actions *right now*, are creating what your future will look like.

8. Amateurs practice so they can get it right. Professionals practice so they never get it wrong.

9. The right solution to the wrong problem is no better than the wrong solution to the right problem.

Chapter 9

SOMETHING THEY CAN BELIEVE IN

There is always a market for offering people something they *can believe in* that is credible. The demand is insatiable.

If, however, in the process of selling, you make statements or claims that seem *incredible,* you will be seen as *not credible,* meaning not believable. This creates an *atmosphere of doubt* that is nearly impossible to recover from. Don't promise them the moon when they already know it's impossible.

Offer them something that is believable and credible and that satisfies their purposes. Then show them a way to get it and you'll have all the sales you can handle.

Edward R. Murrow, American broadcast journalist, known for his honesty and integrity in delivering the news said it this way,

"To be persuasive we must be believable; to be believable we must be credible; *to be credible we must be truthful.*"

THE SUCKER AT THE TABLE

Today was the day of our big presentation for a new, important European client. We were *going all in* for the biggest deal we had ever pitched, confident and prepared to put on our most compelling presentation.

Visions of a new big account in our future and enormous success for our prospective client were dancing in our heads.

But alas, it was not to be.

They hit us with a sucker punch before we even got in the game. It was as embarrassing as it was painful to discover that we were the *sucker at the table.*

Upon review, it became clear how our sales team **was put off their game.** I'll explain.

At the beginning of the meeting, they threw us a curve by insisting upon giving us a general presentation on their company. They said this was *to help us understand* the internal dynamics and policies of their company for securing outside services. Reluctantly, we agreed, as we couldn't really refuse could we? The first of several mistakes we made that day.

They proceeded to spend an hour on a well rehearsed, convincing monologue, which laid out the internal purchasing procedures. They carefully explained why they were firmly limited to only a *certain size budget* for the type of program we were suggesting.

They were also very polite and nice about letting us know why we weren't going to close the big deal that we expected. You could almost hear the wind rushing out of our sails as our hopes of a big deal were summarily crushed.

Their final budget was 50% less than our estimate to accomplish all they wanted. Putting our disappointment aside, after they were done, we got up to begin our presentation and dutifully went through the motions – but it was clear that our hearts were not in it.

They seemed excited at the possibility of doing business with us, but only *if we could just cut a little more out of our price!* We talked it over, and reluctantly swallowed what pride we had left, grudgingly agreeing to shave another 5% off our margin.

In the end, we closed a deal that they were very happy, but . . . *we got skunked.*

I'm certain this process was a template, one that they had rehearsed and drilled many times before meeting with us. We got out sold, clear and simple. In fact, to confirm my feelings, much later I was involved with another presentation with this same company. They pulled the *exact same thing* as the first time I caught their act. They must have thought, the template was working, why change it? And they were right.

Any negotiation tends to go to the side that is better prepared, practiced, and with a definite playbook to follow. They had plans and backup plans and even more contingency plans to cope with anything we came up with. We simply got outplayed by a vastly more experienced and trained group of negotiators.

Without knowing it, we ended up being *the sucker at the table.* The experience was painful and expensive, but we did learn some important lessons that served us in good stead in the future.

1. *Expect the unexpected.*

Never go into any negotiation or closing situation unprepared for anything that could come up. Positive thinking is wonderful, but the side that has *done their homework,* is organized, and has a focused plan with the exact outcome they want, most often comes away the winner.

2. *Time and information are your most powerful tools.*

Conduct a thorough research on the company *before the meeting.* Find out everything you can about them. Why did they contact your company? What are their time constraints? Who is doing the presentation? What do you know about them?

Any information will give you a small edge; *all the information will give you an enormous advantage.*

3. *Don't assume anything.*

If you must assume something, then assume something unexpected will happen. That's a pretty safe bet. If you assume that *anything that could go wrong will go wrong*, and prepare accordingly, you have a chance of staying in the game, and even closing the deal. *That for which you are unprepared, inevitably does happen.*

4. *They want your services as much as you need their business.*

Ignore anything they say to the opposite. They wouldn't be there if they weren't serious about doing business with your company. It's *likely they want you more than you need them.*

Don't feel weak just because they are pretending to be stronger. *Your position is just as strong as theirs, or stronger.*

5. *When you can't spot the sucker at the table, you're it!*

Remember it's a tough, cutthroat game when it gets down to the fine print with big money in play.

If you look around the negotiating table and realize that you're the most inexperienced one there, watch out: you're being set up. And this just may be a painfully expensive lesson for you.

6. *Develop walk-away power.*

This is an important one, and perhaps the most valuable. When you have *walk-away power,* you are negotiating from a position of strength.

When you adopt the attitude that you *just have to have the deal,* you move to the weak side of the negotiations. Even if you really do need the money, it's not your job to worry about it right now; it's the wrong target.

Keep your attention on doing a presentation that they can't refuse and the money will take care of itself.

You will lose a deal now and then, but at least you'll retain your integrity and become known as a *tough, but fair negotiator.*

And that's a lot better than getting a reputation as *the sucker at the table,* isn't it?

STOP, LOOK, LISTEN

Long ago, a trusted friend and mentor gave me an *insider's tip to success.* He took me aside, and in hushed, semi-secretive tones said simply,

"You know, there are only two rules for success in business. The first rule is don't tell everything you know."

As I moved to the edge of my seat anxiously awaiting the revelation of the all-important second rule, he just looked at me with a knowing smile, patiently waiting for the significance of the first rule to sink in.

I finally caught on, to his obvious delight. He wasn't going to tell me rule number two, because if he did, he would have *violated rule number one.*

In this simple exchange, I realized three important lessons:

    a. The value of *speaking* clearly,

    b. The secret of *listening actively,*

    c. The importance of *live communication.*

Further, the consequence of not maintaining a *proper balance* between these three elements may be even more important. New sales people often think they have to become expert at fast-talking to convince the prospect to buy from them. This assumption or preconception is incorrect. To become expert in selling, you have to become an expert in *listening and responding appropriately.* And you can't listen or respond correctly without *being interested* in them.

You may be talking too much – listening too little – and selling less than you could and should be as a result. More often than you may think, you could be talking someone *out of the deal,* rather than getting him or her interested in doing business with you.

Yes, it is commonly accepted in the sales business that you are paid to talk to people, get them interested, to give presentations, generate and present proposals, and close deals.

And all of this requires an almost constant outflow of communication, right?

Well, not exactly.

While you do have to become comfortable and competent in speaking to people, a total focus on this element of the job and a neglect of the other elements will leave you wondering why you aren't closing more contracts. A slight adjustment in the way you approach selling could give you greater returns – and in less time – than you ever imagined.

A master salesperson is one who understands when to speak and when to sit down, shut up, and listen. Famed litigator Alan Dershowitz says the same thing in his own way. "A good lawyer knows how to shut up when he's won his case."

This true story will illustrate.

One very able salesman I know monitors how long he is talking only by whether or not he is getting dizzy while continuing a fire-hose-like approach to his presentation.

Not that he is uninteresting, but the avalanche of words is almost too much for anyone. The audience reaches the point of saturation, and eventually turns off and *stops listening before he stops talking.* Unfortunately, this situation is not uncommon in the sales profession.

Now, it's easy to point fingers at blowhard salesmen from our own experiences as buyers.

For example, the car salesman who talks non-stop through the whole test drive, the unbidden phone solicitor, the open house real estate agent who won't leave you alone for a moment and insists on rapid-fire narrative through the whole tour, etc.

When you try to get a word in edge-wise, it seems these CO_2 machines grudgingly let you blurt out your question or comment, then continue with complete disregard to your concerns. Whatever the individual reasons behind it, it is a very real situation that adversely affects far too many otherwise able salespeople.

But, as with bad breath or body odor, people often don't normally mention it; they just get away as quickly as possible. Unfortunately, some salesmen never realize the value of listening. Why? Because they become *stunted* by an early fluke success.

Every now and then, the sales filibuster approach actually works, as a prospect becomes so spellbound with the "*magical*" presentation before him that he hypnotically signs whatever is put under his pen.

The salesman then credits that experience as the key to his success. But this is nearly the *worst thing that can happen.* As time passes, he still continues working, acting as a green rookie – despite years of experience under his belt – filling every available bit of space with the sound of his own voice.

So what's the answer, anyway?

Well, if you suppress the urge to over-talk, fight back the fears that cause it, and relax, you will begin to really see those presently in front of you.

And, I think you'll agree, they are not threatening in the main.

Instead, they are mostly there to gain something from the interaction with you. You'll find they are usually willing to let you entertain, enlighten, and inspire them – adding a little life to what is often an otherwise dull and ordinary day.

From your position as a potential source of help for them, you have the opportunity to really see what they want, what they are reacting to, positively or negatively, and handle accordingly. There will never be any canned, memorized script that will be a substitute for a real live person communicating to the prospect. This is your big advantage, because most of the people you are talking with have never really been communicated to before.

Live communication (not a canned or memorized script) in the fullest sense of the word, is probably the second most desired element of human interaction. Yet it is so seldom found, that if you can accomplish this in your sales efforts, you will be noticed – if only from the lack of competition in this arena.

You'll be in *rare air,* and stand out from the crowd, that's for sure; and in this over-communicated society, you can use all the help you can get!

The moral is: your likelihood of success is enhanced enormously once you begin communicating *with people,* not just talking at or to them while thinking only of yourself.

Communication is a reciprocal process, a give and take that happens between people who are interested in what someone else is saying.

And if you're not interested in them, I can guarantee that you'll never notice that they've stopped listening long before you stopped talking.

STYLES OF SELLING

My first day on a selling job, many years ago when I was just starting out, consisted of a *sales training program.*

This amounted to one-half day accompanying a *veteran* salesman, going door-to-door calling on prospective customers.

The following day, without even a business card to identify me, I was hired on as a "professional" salesman.

This hiring system worked on a *trial by fire basis, intended* to test your character and ability to perform well under pressure. At the end of your first day selling, you were *either in or you were out.*

So there I was, an intrepid young salesman, walking out the door with my trusty map, a fist-full of "qualified" leads, and a black suitcase full of samples in the trunk of my car.

Armed only with my common sense, a friendly disposition, and a smile, I felt I was as ready as I would ever be.

Plus, I was *excited and interested* (my two greatest assets as it turned out).

Well, to my surprise (and the delight of my sales manager) at the end of the day, I was the top salesman in the office.

The sales manager was so thrilled he got up on his desk (literally), and jumped up and down after seeing the amount of sales I had made. Not an easy feat as he definitely was not a small man.

I admit I liked the attention; but at the same time, it sort of felt like an undeserved validation. After all, I didn't think I had really done any selling, per se.

All I did was find *something I had in common* with the people I met, asked a *few questions,* and then let them talk for as long as they wanted. As I found their stories were interesting, it really wasn't all that hard for me.

Eventually, they would run out of things to say and inevitably ask, "Whatcha got in the suitcase?"

At which time, I'd open it up, show my wares, get out my order form and let them buy what caught their eye. Interestingly, they always bought more than I anticipated. I'd walk out with a big order and they would be smiling, inviting me back any time.

"Hey, this selling business is pretty easy," I thought to myself.

Only later did I discover that my native instincts, while accidently correct, could only take me so far. I needed to know more about the subject of selling if I were to survive in what was a very competitive marketplace. Thus began my quest to learn as much as I could about this subject of selling.

A major part of my discovery process was this: there are *five primary levels of expertise* in the business of selling, from amateur to master. And the path from bottom to top is accomplished over time in a gradual, step-by-step manner, always progressing through these five recognizable styles, outlined below.

The *styles of selling* to follow will allow you to easily side-check your own progress and see what level you're on. Then you can estimate what needs to be done to either strengthen what you're doing right, or correct your weaknesses so you can move forward.

Each one of the styles of selling is followed by the distinctive characteristics of that level. You may find yourself at more than one level, this not uncommon.

To determine which level you should start with, choose the one with which you have the most in common. In this way, your progress forward will be a natural progression toward sales mastery.

Here are the five major selling styles:

Level 1. Amateur

Characteristics: Unskilled, rote script memorization; pushy, frustrated, forced, blames others, inflexible, imitates and copies others in an attempt to emulate their methods; degree of success is sporadic with intermittent success; lacking understanding of why or how methods work. Limited immediate success but potential is positive.

Level 2. Apprentice

Characteristics: Limited skills suitable for common selling situations by imitation of methods of others; rudimentary recognition of fundamentals; beginning to gain some facility with the tools of selling. Requires training and guidance from supervisors to correct efficiencies of time or tools of the trade; needs disciplined and dedicated practice under supervision to move up to the next level.

Level 3. Semi-Pro

Characteristics: The fastest way to achieve this level and move up the levels above is to find and utilize a mentor. They've been through everything you're going through and know the pitfalls and how to avoid them. Before long, you'll be seeing the results from training and practice in sales tools that you dreamed of earlier. You're more relaxed and confident yet disciplined and controlled; not fixed to a certain script; interested and adaptive; you know the fundamentals and you're beginning to develop your own methods with more consistent sales results and referrals; considered reliable in most ordinary sales situations without supervision.

Level 4. Expert

Characteristics: A skilled sales professional; able to apply knowledge of basics of selling in all situations; positive attitude; integrates new knowledge and information easily; interest, certainty, confidence and competence built on consistent demonstrated success; flexible and able to adjust methods to fit the customer; knows the product and can read people; assurance of own abilities and judgment based on achievements; a consistent track record of successful sales; gets referrals easily. Considered among the top 15% of working professionals in the field.

Level. Master

Characteristics: Masters in the art and practice of selling are as valuable as they are rare. Their knowledge and integration of the natural laws of selling is fully assimilated into their own methods of selling. They can think conceptually and are able to change methods to align with customers' needs effortlessly; they can correct the selling process instantly as needed; detect and handle potential problems before they appear; able to develop own methods without violating the natural laws of selling.

They need little or no supervision; they are resourceful and innovative; open to new ideas or methods without changing what is already working; personal initiative and persistence is unstoppable. They are self-starters, self-motivated, friendly, organized, unrushed and unforced; a mature professional attitude and appearance.

They get along well with others; possess natural friendly people skills and abilities. They are highly interested in other people; likeable, sincere and honest. Their sales methods are fresh and unique but rooted in basic, bedrock fundamentals of selling.

They make their own luck by careful preparation and hard work. Their willingness to face and handle difficult situations consistently mystifies others.

They are in the top 2% in company sales statistics; repeat customers ask for this salesperson by name and prefer to deal with this person. They have insouciance, a relaxed and calm state of not worrying about anything, which is infectious. It's a byproduct of a depth of understanding and experience that doesn't happen overnight. It requires a focused, disciplined dedication to master each small step in the overall sales process and then put all these steps to work, effortlessly.

But in doing this, the *seriousness*, common in the attitudes of the neophyte, is a thing of the past. The master has worked hard to get where he or she is, and will wholeheartedly agree with the truth of this statement:

As you become better organized and successful, be prepared for the next weakest point and immediately handle that point.

Continue this sequence until you reach the highest levels, with certainty and stability. The price you pay to reach the top is constant attention to detail, rigorous, ongoing training and disciplined application of your skills, and not abandoning the fundamentals that got you to the top, by constantly strengthening them with great attention to the small details.

Finally, you must enjoy the process as much as you do the result. In this way, you'll have a life and not just a job.

THE TWO-PERCENT CLUB

The 2% Club is that elite group at the very top of any profession, whether recognized as such or not.

Fully understanding the principles and concepts involved to reach these heights in the sales profession takes dedication and persistence, but it's worth it, as the top 2% of salesmen and women who knock down the big commissions and salaries already know.

Like anyone at the top of their game, true professional salespeople live and breathe sales 24/7.

They are either thinking about it, studying about it, practicing it, or directly involved in the activity.

Careful study, focused practice, and correct repetition of the basic skills involved will improve your game and move you toward the top.

You can bet that if you're not doing it, your competition is.

THE AIDA MODEL IS FLAWED

I may step on a few toes with this article, as many salespeople swear by the AIDA (Awareness, Interest, Desire, Action) technique. I'm just not one of them.

Now, if you'll just stay with me for a few minutes, I think it you'll find it will be worth your time.

The opinions in this article are my own, based upon empirical observation and experiences in selling and working with salespeople.

First a little history: The AIDA technique was originated in 1898 by the American advertising and sales pioneer, E. St. Elmo Lewis, with his *Hierarchy of Effects Model.*

He developed this as a practical sales tool based on customer studies in an attempt to explain the *mechanisms of personal selling.*

Lewis held that the most successful salespeople followed a categorized, four layer process using the four cognitive or mental phases that buyers follow when accepting a new idea or purchasing a new product.

The four steps of his AIDA funnel technique are:

1. *Awareness* of the existence of a product or service
2. *Interest* in paying attention to the product's benefits
3. *Desire* for the product
4. *Action toward satisfying the demand*

Lewis held that the fourth stage, or mental state, *action* (purchasing) was a natural result of moving through the first three stages.

For example:

1. *Are you talking to me?* (awareness)
2. *Why are you talking to me?* (interest)
3. *Good idea; but do I really need it?* (desire)
4. *What will I have to do to get it?* (action)

His model is based on the assumption that *external stimuli* from the sales representative are the determining factors by which people become *motivated to* act in purchasing anything.

This theory became accepted in consumer behavior research as the hierarchy of effects model.

It was also widely used by sales managers as the backbone for structuring administration and management of sales activity and results. But, while sales managers welcomed it, customers didn't necessarily share the same viewpoint.

Why? Because this model takes the view that the *salesperson,* rather than the buyer, has the most control in the interaction; an assumption largely refuted by later research.

Also, the model tended to be applied too rigidly, not allowing the flexibility necessary to handle the surprises common in any sale. The problem was that it demanded that the customer fit the sales method rather than allowing the *salesperson to adapt and adjust* to fit the needs of the customer.

This short story will illustrate the point.

Years ago, I supervised a salesman who had been trained in the AIDA funnel technique which he followed religiously, to his and the customer's detriment.

Using this method as a strict template, he talked far more than he listened, apparently attempting to keep the prospect moving through the funnel without objection.

This was problematic because, after directing the prospect through the four steps he would often discover that the customer was not moving into action.

So, he would resort to forcing the close, even *demanding action* from the customer. Then, to no one's surprise, this only created more *resistance*, requiring even more force to seal the deal. On rare occasions it worked, if only poorly. But the customers never forgot how it made them feel and certainly weren't anxious to repeat the experience.

Now, I admit that the work of Lewis and the AIDA funnel method is commendable as a starting point in selling and examining the mechanics of selling, but something was overlooked in the process. What's missing is *the human factor.*

It may have looked good on paper, but it mostly failed in practice. Why? Because all selling is based on the *human activity* of exchanging products and services for *mutual benefit.*

To assume you can leave the customer out of the equation and still believe there will be a mutual benefit is *unsound thinking*. It exposes an *incomplete understanding* of the way people work in the real world.

In fact, this method violates this basic law selling:

Law: All selling is based on mutual agreement.

Agreement is based on things you have in common with people. You cannot force someone to agree with you.

The primary requisite to understanding selling is to first understand people. You cannot separate these two elements and hope to achieve consistent results. They are opposite sides of the same coin. Any attempt to quantize the human activity of selling to make it fit into a mechanical schematic with little boxes and connected lines will ultimately fail.

People are not trained animals or animated robots, as much as some self-proclaimed experts would like to think otherwise.

People can, and do, act and react in some very unpredictable ways that may not align with your techniques, methods and tactics, no matter how well thought out.

You have to *adjust your methods so they align with the customer*, not force them to adapt to you.

Only by realizing that you're dealing with another live human being, with their own feelings, desires, problems, fears, needs and wants, will you have any chance whatsoever of forming a relationship with that customer or prospect. And until you can do that, you will make only *accidental sales*. By which I mean those in which another salesperson, at some earlier time, did all the prep work to create a relationship with the person and interested them in the product.

And now you are receiving the benefit of that work.

The AIDA funnel method is, however, crudely workable, as it does outline some of the general levels that all customers move through in the purchasing process.

But it omits the most important factor: the people generally and the *individual*, specifically.

But until those levels from *awareness to action* are aligned with the natural laws of selling, *common to all people*, this method is no better than any other odd-ball technique or tactic.

You're always far better off looking to the basic underlying laws of selling to build your career on, as these are laws that will *never let you down*.

THE ANCESTOR OF ACTION

"The ancestor of every action is a thought." - Ralph Waldo Emerson

This quotation is consistent with much of my writing on the concept of creating action and sales results. I would only add one thing to this quote: in my observations and experience, prior to any action, there are three separate factors involved: *attention, thought and emotion.* And all three precede action.

Something has to attract your attention to get the process started. For example, you see an ad on TV for a big pizza or some hot wings and it gets your attention.

Even if you were feeling hungry before you saw the ad, now you have the thought, "*I'm hungry*," and at nearly the same time, experience the emotion of what it feels like to satisfy that hunger; then you feel motivated to satiate that need and go into action to do it.

Why? It's simple: Your attention directs your thoughts. Your thoughts stimulate your emotions. Your emotions trigger and activate the body to go into action.

This action was preceded by, and motivated by your attention (curiosity), thought (mentally imagining something), and emotion (feeling what it would be like).

Whatever the initial cause, your attention directed your thoughts and your thoughts triggered your emotions, which motivated your action to satisfy your hunger.

Yes, *the ancestor of action is thought* as long as you include attention and emotion into the mix as well.

Law: Attention influences thoughts. Thoughts influence emotions.

THE ART OF OBSERVATION

Sir William Osler, the eminent professor of medicine at Oxford University, once stated,

"There is no more difficult art to acquire than the art of observation."

I agree, adding only that the difficulty in acquiring this art may only be surpassed by its importance.

This brief story provides a lesson on the art and skill of observation that can dramatically improve your sales, instantly.

Read carefully:

A small bottle sat upon the desk of Sir Osler. Sitting before him was a class full of young, wide-eyed medical students.

The subject of the lecture that day was the art of observation. To emphasize his point, he announced:

"This bottle contains a urine sample for analysis. It's often possible by tasting it to determine the disease from which the patient suffers, if we observe details."

Then he dipped a finger into the fluid and brought it into his mouth.

He continued speaking:

"Now I am going to pass the bottle around. Each of you please do exactly as I did. Perhaps we can learn the importance of this technique and diagnose the case."

The bottle made its way from row to row, each student gingerly poking his finger in and bravely sampling the contents with a frown.

Dr. Osler then retrieved the bottle and startled his students by saying:

"Gentlemen, now you will understand what I mean when I speak about details. Had you been observant, you would have seen that I put my INDEX FINGER in the bottle but my MIDDLE FINGER into my mouth!"

Those students learned a lesson that day that they would never forget. *And neither should you.*

The art of correct observation is a skill that can be learned. It is a function of attentive watching, paying careful attention, and noting the results.

Whether the observation is after the fact or during the action is a factor of time. The importance and value of the art of observation stands alone. Its value requires no further proof; it is a self-evident fact.

When your sales efforts seem to be rough and failing, step back and take a *careful look*. What are you missing? Have you misidentified the correct source of your troubles? And most importantly, *are you really observing correctly?* The art of and practice of correct observation is the most important asset in any sales activity. Everything flows from this fundamental principle.

That which you can observe, you can control and do something about. That which you cannot observe, can control you and you can do nothing to change it.

That which you cannot face, will give you trouble; this is guaranteed. In sales, you cannot substitute a rote routine, script, technique or method for a real, live willingness and ability to observe correctly and still expect to succeed.

I assure you, practicing the art and discipline of observing what is in front of you will pay off beyond your wildest dreams.

There are many, many ways to sell, but wrap your wits around *the art of observation* and everything else becomes easier and more effective.

THE BASICS OF SELLING

In job interviews for prospective salespeople, I was always surprised at how few knew anything about the fundamentals of selling, despite past successes. *Now, operating on the concept that words have meaning and actions have consequences, there is a benefit to knowing exactly what the word "selling" means.*

To begin, 'selling' is an action verb. And as such, we need a definition that incorporates this fact.

So, here is an *action definition of selling:*

The action of causing a communication between the seller and the buyer that will increase the desire, enhance value, and facilitate a willing exchange to the benefit of both parties.

Note that there are six key words in the above definition.

The key words:

1. causing
2. communication
3. desire
4. value
5. exchange
6. benefit

And the meaning of each of the key words, as follows:

Causing: The actions of bringing about or making something happen; bringing into being or being responsible for a certain result.

Communication: The activity of conveying thoughts, feelings, and information; from the Latin word communis – meaning *to have in common or to share.*

Desire: To want something very strongly; a *wish, need or longing* for something.

Value: The *perception of worth,* importance, or usefulness of something to somebody.

Exchange: To give something and receive something of value in return.

Benefit: A personal consideration of help or advantage.

The potential benefit resulting from a complete understanding of each of these words (*communication, cause, desire, value, exchange, benefit*) should not be taken lightly.

As within the definitions of these key words you can discover all the basics of selling.

Time spent studying them to achieve a working understanding will put you securely on the bedrock of the fundamentals.

Chapter 10

THE BRIDGES TO SALES SUCCESS

Did you know that there are bridges to success in selling? Yep, there are. Read on and all will be revealed.

Have you ever met a salesperson that is the master of finding leads? One who could find a prospect during the dry season in the Gobi Desert?

How about the guy they call Golden Throat? Get him on a sales call and he'll make a good pitch to sell feathers to a goose.

And what about the salesman who lives to *close deals*? He's not long on getting leads or product knowledge, but boy can he hammer it when he smells a close!

While I agree that in some corporate selling environments, you don't have to worry about cold calls, a smooth pitch, or infallible closing techniques, still, most salesmen I know resemble one of the above.

And that's a shame.

Why? Because, *they're losing sales.* Each of these three archetypes represents one of the bridges that transport potential clients from one stage (island, if you will) of the sales process to the next, and finally to the close.

The problem we encounter is that the professional salesperson has to be proficient at building all the bridges, not just one or two.

It is the rare pro that has the whole package. But that doesn't mean it's impossible – or even difficult to achieve.

In fact, all that's required is to gain an awareness of the natural laws of selling and develop methods that align with them.

So, let's look at these bridges one at a time, and then see how they all fit together in accomplishing our aims.

The Terrain

If you examine the process as a whole, you will recognize the discrete stages of a successful sale:

a) Unnoticed Product Existence – No market or potential leads yet.

b) Awareness of Product – Your potential clients or markets are aware of your product.

c) Thorough Knowledge of Product – Your prospect is fully informed about the advantages, personal benefits, and potential profits connected with your product.

d) The Close – The prospect signs on the deal. He has graduated to become a client.

Each stage exists as a sort of resting place, but it's also where the prospect can potentially become stalled.

The bridges are more important than the stages themselves, as this is where they can feel uncomfortable.

It's your job to create curiosity and interest in the next bridge and make it as comfortable as possible in doing so.

Next, we'll explore exactly how to make and cross those bridges for the prospect so you can lock in the sale.

The process usually starts with the fact that you have a product or service, but no prospects to sell to.

How do you get out of that lonesome state of nonexistence? You must somehow first attract the attention of the prospect to you and your product to have any possibility of a sale. Here are the bridges to be crossed.

Capturing Attention

*This is the **first bridge*** you must cross in the sales process. So, let's see if we can break it down to its simple basics as a starting point of agreement.

The dictionary defines the word "attention" as an observation with a view to action and the act of bringing something into clear awareness.

Awareness, then, is the operative word here.

The goal is to create an *awareness of your product or service.*

If the public is unaware of your products or services, by definition, you simply don't exist for them, whatever the real value of your product or service.

You could say that this first broad target is *awareness creation,* and you would be right.

How do you carry this out?

In the beginning, just get something out there. Get more visible; engage people visually; talk to more people; offer a free seminar, an introductory package, a test drive, anything to capture their attention.

Then as you can afford it, upgrade your promotion and advertising to produce the highest quality message possible, within your resources.

However, you accomplish this; *get something out there.* You must be visible to prospects or you simply don't exist on their radar. Note that in our paradigm, no actual selling has yet transpired. To this point, we're just trying to increase awareness so that you won't go unnoticed.

This crucial step provides the foundation for future efforts and must be firmly established by whatever effective means. The good news is that gaining attention is often the easiest bridge to construct.

When you have delivered the customer to a state of awareness of your product and you, you're still a far cry from selling or finally closing them. You must now *develop the interest* that you created with the attention grabber.

Excite Interest

The **second bridge** is the beginning of what we commonly consider sales activity when you give your sales presentation, answer and ask questions, solve problems, and convey your product's benefits.

The dictionary defines *interest* as a feeling of wanting to know, see, do, or own; also, it's the *arousal of such a feeling.*

Of keynote in the above is that interest is a *feeling.*

There is an old saying that if you want people to remember what you say, make them feel something.

I agree. And the easiest way to do this in selling is to *tell a good story* that relates to them.

A well-crafted and delivered story can evoke an emotional connection that is unforgettable. All great salespeople are also great storytellers.

It is the story that provides the human, emotive factor that allows customers to relate to what you're selling.

This takes what you're selling out of the logic or rational plane and into the emotional.

A well-worn sales maxim says it this way,

Talk and they'll walk. Tell, and you'll sell.

Stories are a way to develop the relationship, enhance interest, and turn on the desire.

If they don't desire what you're offering, it has no value. Value depends directly to how much they desire it and on no other significant factor.

Okay, then what will heat up desire?

When the prospect begins to imagine a personal benefit from what you're offering.

If you can ignite that spark of personal benefit, they not only desire it, now they want it. Yes, telling a good story really is that important. But there is still a third bridge to cross.

Turn On The Emotion

This is the **third bridge**. After you've crossed the first two bridges of *capturing attention and developing interest,* it takes something more to seal the deal.

You can tell when you haven't turned on the emotion when you hear things like this:

"I really appreciated you coming here."

"It's apparent that you really know your material."

"You make a lot of sense."

"I got a lot out of your presentation."

This is because you haven't built and led the prospect across that third and final bridge.

You did not move the prospect to action, specifically, the action of signing at the bottom of the contract.

What went wrong?

This third bridge is *emotion* - based on a natural law of selling: People buy emotionally, and justify it logically.

A classic sales mistake is to try to do the reverse, i.e., motivate the prospect with logic. But it just doesn't work that way.

You've already thrown all the ingredients into the pot — the advantages, benefits, and profit potential — so how come it doesn't turn to soup? Because you have to turn on the heat – *the emotion.* As the emotional temperature rises, the prospect will make his decision to buy.

Then he will seize upon the logic and knowledge you've provided for him and begin to rationalize the inevitable discomfort he is feeling from having to part with his money.

People act and react emotionally, in many unpredictable and peculiar ways, and any of these can affect their buying decisions.

It is your job to think quickly on your feet so you can adapt to and harness these emotions to your advantage. Emotion is the bridge between thinking about doing something and actually going into action.

Law: Emotion creates motion.

Here is the formula: *If they see it, they'll feel it. When they feel it, they'll buy it.*

This is, in fact, a key factor in creating a decision to go into action toward a close.

The car sales rep that says merely, "This is a special gas shock absorber/ wishbone suspension system", ends up with nothing because logic doesn't make them feel anything.

While the one who says, "you'll feel like a king riding in this baby," is much more likely to get the sale because it engages them emotionally. Trust, help, confidence, certainty, conviction, benefits, advantages, price, profits, long-term relationships – these, and more, can be *emotional issues*, not purely analytical ones, if presented the right way.

The *emotional bridge* has to be established. You have to connect with customers in some way that is harmonious with their concerns and purposes.

Top sales people have a superior knowledge of their product or service. But they also have an extremely high degree of conviction that what they offer is also the best solution for the client to help them meet their goals.

They are emotional about it. They're excited about helping the client. Their attitude is enthusiastic and free from doubt. It is unstoppable. It's also very contagious!

As mentioned early, if they don't feel it, they won't buy it. The choice seems clear. Which would you prefer?

No Salesman Is An Island
Remember the salesman archetypes presented at the outset of this article?

Each represents many, many people in the sales business. Each of them is an expert at bridging one of the three gaps in the sales process.

But invariably, they do not succeed as fully as they could and should, because they are not adept at building *all of the bridges.*

The Dead-Eye Closer misses out on potential clients because he doesn't promote his product to find the leads in the first place.

Old Golden Throat drops the ball when it's time to touch just the right emotional chord in the prospect to make him sign.

The Tireless Cold Caller sheds perfectly good leads like a cat does fur because he doesn't develop the interest he's created with his attention grabber.

Sure, they all do get sales. That is because, occasionally, by some means outside their influence, the bridges all get built anyway and enough momentum is established to close the sale.

But for every one they get, a dozen slip away.

It doesn't have to be that way.

An awareness of the three bridges of sales and marketing, and then proper implementation of them, will keep most every sale on track and progressing steadily until it finally comes home for the close.

This could be called a *fourth bridge* but it is really just the culmination of the previous three bridges. This is where we move the prospect into action. How do we do this? You ask for the order.

We crossed the first three bridges by 1) capturing the customer's attention, 2) exciting the interest, and 3) turning on the emotion.

And finally, on this last bridge we move them into action by 4) asking for the order.

Law: You'll never get the order you don't ask for.

No matter how expert your marketing activity, how practiced your sales presentation, how impressive your skills, how slick and glib your carefully learned closing techniques, all would come to naught unless you actually could get something done – ask for the order and close the deal.

It's really not that hard if you've done your work on the previous steps. But skip one of the earlier points, neglect or ignore what customers were really telling you, and sealing the deal is like pulling teeth without an anesthetic. It is painful for you and for them.

And the more you seek to force the issue at the close, the more they seem to dig in and resist even harder.

Not a pretty picture.

To recap, we have now established the *first four pillars* necessary to support our bridge.

Master each of these four discrete areas and your prospects will know you exist, they'll be interested in what you're offering, they'll want your product, and they'll know it's valuable.

And happily, they'll willingly generate the energy necessary to get it.

TALKING THEM OUT OF THE DEAL?

My prospect walked out without saying a word, and the look of disapproval from the sales manager confirmed my own thoughts of inadequacy and failure. Maybe I just wasn't cut out for this line of work.

Evidently, "I was *a talking customer out of the deal,*" at least that is what my supervisor emphatically claimed.

The customer had come in, interested and qualified, and after talking with me, left to find another dealer. I had lost another sale and my job was on the line. I *had* to figure out what I was doing wrong.

On the advice of my supervisor, I made an appointment to talk with the company's new sales consultant. I knew it was time to change something; I just had to find out what it was!

Well, when I met him, I knew something was different. He didn't talk down to me or just point out what I was doing wrong. He was *genuinely interested* in me, and what I had to say. He listened while I vented my frustrations over my inadequacies.

Then to my surprise, he wanted to know *what I was doing right*, in addition to the things that I wanted to change. The more we talked, the more I found my confidence growing. It was clear this was his way of getting me *on my mettle* – by focusing on my strengths and improving my ability to cope with what I needed to handle. And it was working.

With some subtle but deft guidance, I was able to see what was causing me a lot of trouble.

First, I had always been taught to just *get the customer behind the wheel,* and the deal would close automatically. Dutifully, I had been following this advice, but it *wasn't working*.

The consultant pointed out that any prospective sale starts out with a delicate potential connection between the sales rep and the customer, something that is easily broken and hard to repair.

Establishing a **line of trust** first is the *most important* place to focus my attention before trying to get a prospect to do anything.

Further, he said that trust was something that can't be forced. It is either freely given or it doesn't exist – and it can't be rushed; it takes as long as it takes to develop it.

It dawned on me that by ignoring the vital steps of getting the customer to know me and trust me first, I was reversing the natural order of things and *creating resentment* that wasn't there in the first place. Now, that made sense, and was something I could use.

Second, I began to see that I was mostly thinking about *me first* and the *prospect last.*

It should have been the reverse. I had been putting the cart before the horse there, too. By shifting this to thinking about the customer first, I had my priorities in order.

If I were *interested* in the customer, they would tell me how they wanted to be sold. If I were only interested in myself, I'd miss all the signals that told me how to close the deal.

No wonder my prospects had been drifting off without saying a word. I had been *creating my own problems* by only thinking about myself, not really being interested in them.

Third: I had been *forcing my prospects* to fit my mold rather than adjusting to what they were telling me they needed and wanted.

I was *creating resistance* that wasn't there to begin with.

Forth: I saw how I could control the sales process, rather than letting it control me. I didn't have to follow some rote, robotic procedure.

Instead, I could adjust my sales process depending on what the customer was telling me they wanted, but only if I was interested and listening to what they told me. Maybe I was in the right profession after all.

THE CRUCIAL ELEMENT

The following quote is spot on the money:

"The salesman is the crucial element that makes it all work." – Elbert Hubbard

I like his words about the salesman as the crucial element. I also wholeheartedly agree with his idea that the qualities of initiative and responsibility are essential to success. In fact, any formula for sales success must include these two elements:

a) Knowledge and skill of the craft, and the art of selling,

b) The personal characteristics of initiative and responsibility.

There have been tomes of material written about sales techniques, methods, and practices, but comparatively little about the other vital elements of initiative and responsibility.

I think that this may be one of the *hidden reasons* why some sales methods and techniques fail. Because, it's axiomatic that if a natural law is misapplied or not applied at all, you can predict trouble for the future.

And when or if the factors of personal initiative and individual responsibility are absent, success also becomes a pipe dream.

Okay, if it is that important, what do these words mean?

Initiative means: the ability to *act first or on one's own.* It comes from the word *initiate,* which means to begin or set in motion.

Responsibility means: to be *answerable for an act* or its consequences.

It comes from the word *responsible,* which means being a *primary cause* of some event or action; able to be trusted.

These two ingredients are interdependent and mutually supportive in symbiotic fashion. If either element is missing or applied incorrectly, the other will be adversely affected as well.

To put these two concepts to work for you, first carefully study the two definitions, and then ruthlessly seek out any weak spots in yourself in either initiative or responsibility. Once you've isolated the problem area, use self-discipline to correct it and get back on the right track again.

THE EDGE OF SIMPLICITY

Question: How can you tell when you don't understand something well enough? Answer: *Try explaining it to a four or five-year-old child.*

If you can't explain something simply enough for them to understand, you don't understand it either. You may be on *the* edge of simplicity, but you're not there yet.

You need more practice or more experience or both. And, what's worse, *you're losing sales because of this.*

If customers are left with the idea that you may know what you're talking about, but it's too complicated for them to understand, they won't be able to come to a decision.

If clients can easily grasp the simple basics of your message and easily see the benefit for them, you're on the right path.

It's a self-evident principle: Before they can decide, they must understand. A confused prospect cannot decide - and if they can't decide, they won't buy.

This is a problem because people would prefer to make no decision at all, rather than make the wrong one. And no decision at all equals no sale for you.

Sometimes we focus too much on the features, advantages, and benefits and too little about the basics of what we're selling. Instead, strip it back to the fundamentals and practice saying it in a way that aligns with their purposes and is easily understandable. Then the whole process is easier on them and on you.

You are the one responsible for communicating your message in a way that can be understood. If they don't understand, *do not ask for whom the bell tolls, as it tolls for thee.* (With a nod to John Donne)

All truths are basically simple . . . including this one.

Law: If they don't understand, they can't decide. And if they can't decide, they won't buy.

THE FIRST LAW OF SUCCESS

Growing up as a boy in a farm community in Northern Michigan, I was exposed to a work ethic that became a guiding principle in my life. I worked on a farm owned and operated by my Grandfather and my Uncle during the summers. I learned that there are things that *had to be done*, no matter how I feel, what the weather is like, or anything else.

I had to discipline myself to do the chores without excuses. Animals had to be fed, there were cows that had to be milked, pigs, chickens, horses and much more, from dawn to dusk, every day without exception; and putting things off, making excuses, looking for reasons to explain why something didn't get done, was a foreign concept.

I figured out that life is *one big attention magnet* to distract you away from what you really want to do, or should be doing. I also found, that once I made up my mind to show up, I would get something done.

This is when I discovered this law:

Law: The first law of success is **to show up.**

I wasn't the smartest, most talented, best looking, or strongest kid in my community. But I discovered that if I could keep working at something longer than others, I would eventually master whatever I was interested in.

Much later in life, I discovered that others thought much the same way that I did about things like showing up, self-discipline, and persistence.

For example, in an interview for "The Collider" (2008) director, actor and comedian, Woody Allen, put it this way; saying it was the *biggest life lesson* that has worked for him:

"Eighty percent of success is showing up. You really have to discipline yourself to do the work. If you want to accomplish something you can't

spend a lot of time hemming and hawing, putting it off, making excuses for yourself, and figuring ways. You have to actually do it."

Here are a couple more good quotes that support the concept:

"Inspiration is for amateurs. The rest of us *just show* up and get to work." —Chuck Close.

"I've found that luck is quite predictable. If you want more luck, take more chances. Be more active. *Show up* more often." – Brian Tracy.

But what does it really mean to *show up?*

It just means *to stop hiding* and *stop pretending* you're invisible or trying to go unnoticed. You can pretend about many things, but *pretending to show up*, while not being interested in where you are and what's going on should not be one of them.

If you're there, really be there, be yourself and participate; don't just stand around observing or being a spectator in your own life. Answer your phone calls personally, be interested in people, open a conversation and make a contribution, answer your letters or email, go to that meeting or party, accept the invitation to speak and stick around afterwards and talk to people.

Showing up is all about being *interested and contributing*. And I can guarantee that you'll never amount to much in the game of selling if you don't.

It's easier than you think and the more you practice it the easier and more natural it becomes. And soon, doors of opportunity open for you that you didn't even know existed.

It's all pretty simple once you decide to just show up.

One thing more . . . If all you're doing is looking for a *reason not to show up*, you can always find one. But why bother? Why not just show up instead?

You've got nothing to lose except your invisibility and ultimate failure. Just show up, contact, engage and get into communication with people. Train yourself to say YES, instead of your usual response of *maybe sometime, or we'll see.*

Get off the fence. Stop pretending. Either you're interested in success or you're not. If you are, then do what you've got to do to make it happen. Further, if you work at it, you will see desirable changes in every other aspect of your life.

All this and more can be yours . . . but first you must **show up for the game.**

GIRL IN THE WINDOW PRINCIPLE

My long-time friend, Wm. Newman, was enthusiastically telling me about his trip to Amsterdam – a city known for its free-spirited liberalism, diversity and tolerance – when in the blink of an eye, it hit me.

What he was describing was one of the oldest and most effective sales and marketing tools ever developed. Here it is: You must *capture attention and excite imagination* if you can ever expect to close a deal,

This is what I call: *The Girl In The Window Principle.*

Attention or thought marketing, the latest buzz in sales and marketing circles, has been around for ages – since political posters were painted on the walls of the arena in ancient Rome. But these girls in the windows of Amsterdam have it down to a science. Struggling to make a living in an extremely competitive market, the girls realize one thing:

They first have to attract attention then invite the prospect to *imagine the benefits* of doing business together. Here's how they do it.

The Dutch term for this activity is *raambordellen.* It's a word to describe the legal practice of window prostitution, where girls – attempting to attract potential clients – pose visibly and scantily clad in large windows of small rooms in houses along the streets of the Rosse Buurt, one of the red-light districts of Amsterdam.

Regardless of ones' personal opinion of such things, to expect to attract business, the *girl in the window* first *had to capture the attention of prospective clients. Then somehow get the prospect to imagine a personal benefit of doing business together.*

Now hold on to your hat, because here is something that might change your whole outlook on selling. I'm going to show you how to *instantly* attract someone's attention. It's simple: *Give them something they didn't expect.*

The element of surprise is the key to attracting *curiosity, interest and attention.* Of course, this comes from this natural law of selling: *People have an abiding love of surprise.* Show them, tell them, or give them something they never expected or thought of before and you will get their attention. In fact, you won't be able to keep their attention away from it.

What you do next it is up to you. But if you can also engage them further you're on your way to a closed deal. It's pretty much common sense once you look at it. Show them how *they can have what they want* and they'll move mountains to get it. It's no coincidence that every sales or marketing activity follows these same *seven essential steps:*

1. Surprise stimulates curiosity

2. Curiosity attracts attention

3. Attention activates interest

4. Interest excites imagination

5. Imagination initiates desire

6. Desire generates demand

7. Demand seals the deal

Sometimes you come upon a gemstone in the most unexpected places; that is, if you're looking for it.

THE GOAL OF ALL SELLING

The goal of all selling is a simple, fundamental principle: *To help people, to add value,* and agree upon a mutually beneficial product or service for valuable exchange.

Whether in the form of a written or verbal contract, it results in a willing exchange of money for services or products. This is what you're trying to do.

You're trying to build an *agreement* that serves the interests of all parties involved. How you are going to do it is the subject covered under the broad title of methods, which are countless.

You would be well served to spot-check yourself from time to time to make sure you haven't adopted some method that *violates* some basic principles, as this is the path to disaster.

The road to happiness and success is where your methods align with and support your principles.

If your methods are in agreement with your principles, you won't have to *justify, explain or make excuses* for what you're doing.

It's just naturally right, because it's based on the *natural laws of selling.* And that's how you know you're on the right track.

HIERARCHY OF IMPORTANCES IN SELLING

Experience shows that some things are more important than others in selling. Following is a list of elements, in order of importance, which are essential for consistent success in selling.

Use this as a quick mental warm-up you can use to sharpen your focus before you get in the game.

1. Why are you selling?

2. What are you selling?

3. What are you paid for?

4. What is the final result you're looking for?

5. Do you trust yourself as a salesperson?

6. Do you like what you're doing?

7. Are you providing value or just getting paid?

8. Did you show up, ready for work?

9. What do you have in common with them?

10. Are you making a friend while selling?

11. Are they confident you're trying to help?

12. Can you capture their attention?

13. What will excite their imagination?

14. Have you found their purpose for buying?

15. Does your solution solve their problem?

16. Is what you're selling the best for them?

17. Can they see the benefit of your product?

18. Are you trying to sell two things at once?

19. Are you talking instead of listening?

20. Did you skip an earlier step?

21. Is your paperwork in order?

22. Can you deliver what you've promised?

23. Are they still smiling after the deal is sealed?

24. Did you get paid?

25. Are they willing to tell others about you (favorably)?

THE HUMAN FACTOR

What makes something valuable? Why is it that the worth, importance, or usefulness of something to somebody – is more valuable than anything else?

It is well known that value is a *personal consideration*, like beauty, and that it lies in the eye of the beholder. But there are other factors to consider.

The first factor is *perception.*

Perception is the process of becoming aware of the world around you through your senses.

But, human nature being what it is, not everyone is prepared to see what is in front of him or her, as Ralph Waldo Emerson correctly said with this quote,

"People only see what they are prepared to see."

So, a large part of your job is to increase awareness, of you, your company, your products or services.

Awareness through the senses plays a critical role in *perception* and behavior.

Perception is awareness, but the same object or event can be perceived very differently depending upon your point of view.

This is why perception, in and of itself, does not make something real. Something else is required.

The second factor is *reality.*

In the physical universe, reality is what is real, it exists physically, it can be weighed, measured, and otherwise verified as existing as a fact, not imagination.

But if you and I both *agree* that something is valuable or important, or useful, or "real" - then at least to us, it is. That commonality makes something more real between the two of us. If others also concur, then the consensus of opinion becomes stronger and more expansive.

Whether something is valuable in fact, is immaterial. That we agree that something is valuable is *what makes it real to us* as *beauty is in the eye of the beholder.*

But every salesperson must know this law: *agreement is the keynote of all selling.*

These two factors of perception (awareness) and reality (agreement) explain a large part of why anything is considered valuable.

But there is yet one more.

The third is the *human factor.*

We all make decisions based on the human factor of self-preservation. This is based upon a natural law of survival, shared by all human beings. But while we all have this ingredient in common, that's where the similarity ends.

The choices we make in pursuing our individual route toward survival are dramatically different for each person. This is where the *human factor* enters the picture.

The human factor is, in fact, the *catalyst* that *activates* the other two elements of perception and reality.

The human factor is what *creates want* – which is the strongest force there is in impelling action.

Once we become aware that some product or service will enhance our lives and benefit the lives of others, this becomes a motivating force of desire and want. We make these choices of *relative worth*, based upon perception (awareness) and reality (agreement).

The human factor is the *glue that creates want.*

Perception and reality, plus the human factor, create want; it's the combination of all three elements that *create the magic.*

What makes it unique is that a change in any one point invariably affects the other two – to your advantage or not.

When any one of the three factors of *perception, reality or want* is missing, the sale will not reach a close. When all three are in evidence, the customer *will demand* what you're offering. And they will *insist* that you provide it to them. Now, all you have to do is give them what they want. This is not based on my opinion. These three factors are obvious to any that care to look.

All you have to do is understand the terms (perception, reality, want) and see how they fit into your immediate situation. Practice applying it until it becomes as natural as rain and it will reap greater rewards than ever imagined.

A quote from author Richelle E. Goodrich supports this tidbit of wisdom with her own writing:

"Do it again. Play it again. Sing it again. Read it again. Write it again. Sketch it again. Rehearse it again. Run it again. Try it again. Because *again* is practice, and practice is improvement, and improvement only leads to perfection."

THE INFLUENCERS

C-level executives (Chief Executive Officer, Chief Operations Officer, Chief Financial Officer, etc.) are called *the influencers* for good reason. They're at the top of the food chain and are always interested in everything that is going on in their company, and are especially what the competition is up to; unlike accountants and lawyers, who only think in numbers or in words, *top executives think in concepts.*

They also have the will and the determination to put *ideas it into action.* They deal in futures. These are the ones who bring about a *sea change* (substantial transformation) for the better in any business they work with. Further, they didn't get that position by sitting around waiting for the phone to ring.

They are actively involved all the time and they prioritize their time and attention carefully so as not to waste this valuable resource. That's how they became known as "The Influencers."

So, if you want to make an impression, you have to get in the right frame of mind to talk to them. This means take off your shoes and imagine what it's like to walk a mile in theirs.

Look at what he or she has to contend with from their viewpoint. Imagine what it would be like if you were approached by someone you didn't know, eating up your time, trying to sell you something you probably aren't interested in.

What would be your reaction? You'd be *resistive,* of course, just like they are. So what would get their attention? *You have to surprise them.*

Give them something they didn't expect; a new look at the market, a fresh idea for marketing, something they haven't thought of yet.

Just like you, they will always be *interested* in something that will help them solve their problems – and their problems concern things like: what the competition is up to; increasing profits and market share: new product developments, cutting costs.

And did I mention . . . the competition?

Also like anyone else, they respond to a *good story*. Make it real, interesting and relevant – and remember to keep it brief and simple, with a heavy dose of humanity.

The hot tip here is that the *element of surprise* is what will get their attention. Then follow up with something that will ignite their imagination. This will hit them where they live.

And after all, as these are the people who can say "Yes" when others can only say "No" – they can make things a lot easier for you.

Just remember that you have to **step into their shoes** to see things as they do. If you can, you'll get their attention. If you can't, you'll get the door.

Don't underestimate the power of this seemingly simple concept.

THE MAGIC BUTTON

Let's say, for example, that you're in the middle of your presentation – you feel the time is right for a close and you push your magic button *guaranteed* to close the sale.

But it falls flat and doesn't work. What do you do now? Well, if that's all you've got in your arsenal, you're going to walk away empty-handed.

Subjected to various socioeconomic, financial and political pressures of life, people don't always follow the script you have prepared. And, as my Aunt Virginia always said, "the only thing you can totally count on is that *things will change,*" which is a natural law in itself:

Law: Things will change.

When dealing with people your success depends on how well you can adapt your tactics to the inevitability of unexpected changes.

Law: You can never predict with 100% accuracy what people will think, say or do.

You have to be on your toes and if you are unable to adjust, adapt and align your efforts to them instantly, there is something else you can always count on – you will not make the sale. It can be frustrating.

But now I'm going to let you in on a secret. Customers don't have one button – *they have dozens.*

But there is one "magic go button" that underlies all the rest. If used correctly, it can become a stabilizing factor in all other methods and tactics of selling.

You just have to follow this instruction:

Find more ways for them to say "Yes" than they have to say "No." No matter what else you do, using the wrong tool for the job will lead to very difficult and unsatisfying results (for you and the customer). So, where do you find the 'right' buttons to use?

This is an excellent question, one to which everyone seems to have his or her own pat answer. They'll tell you their theories on which buttons work best, but mostly you'll learn the right buttons from your own experience.

There is no substitute for getting face to face with a prospect to show you what works and what doesn't.

Gradually, by trial and error, you build up a stockpile of 'buttons' to use when appropriate. Your success ratio increases and your confidence builds, and you're on your way. But doesn't this take a lot of time and effort? Yes, but it's worth it.

So, for those of you that still hold out hope for that one magic button that will produce instantaneous changes for you, I have the answer.

As mentioned, there are more than two magic buttons, but these two are of major importance.

Magic Button #1: *Get people to like you and trust you.*

This is, in fact, the open-sesame to each subsequent step in your sales process. Yes, I know, words are easy to say and hard to put into action, but that doesn't alter the truth of the statement. Happily, there is a surefire route that will help you achieve this.

This next one is a gemstone and it's as obvious as it is powerful.

Magic Button #2: *Honestly trust and like yourself first.*

If there is anything that will set the stage for your long-term happiness and success in sales and in life, it is this: They'll like you and trust you *when you like and trust yourself.*

Although this button is second, arguably it is the most important and it is something only you can do. When the philosopher, Diogenes, searched the world looking for *one honest man* he was not far off the mark. Being honest with yourself first is what puts you on the road to being honest with others. If you're not truthful to yourself, you're untruthful to others as well, and you're doing both of you a disservice.

When you're honest with yourself, you can be honest with others.

If you trust yourself, others will trust you.

Your internal attitudes about yourself put in motion a whole series of factors, for better or for worse.

A positive attitude about yourself will change your tone of voice, your smile, your physical bearing, the way you look and the way others see you. The reverse is also true.

So, the ball is in your court. If you're serious about succeeding, then step up and really look at you. Face up to your strengths and weaknesses. We all have them.

If you can do this, you have reached the first step of becoming honest with yourself and with others. And incidentally, you will have opened the door to a stress-free life and a successful career.

It turns out that this old saying by Mark Twain still applies:

"When in doubt, tell the truth."

Chapter 11

THE MIND'S EYE

This brief article will take a closer look will reveal something that is applicable to all selling activities.

Read carefully, and all will become clear to you.

It is human nature to take something for granted when we did nothing to attain it. The *power of the mind's eye* is one of these things.

It's something we all have, but fail to acknowledge or use to full advantage.

This, the essence of creative imagination employs an ability to visualize how something could or should be, combined with a willingness and resourcefulness to make it so.

But, when our attention is fixed on what has been or what is, we cannot imagine *what could be*. And futures belong in the *what-if or what could be* category

Artists of all types are among those rare individuals who can recognize the value of vision, imagination and intelligent foresight, and put these elements to use. And they are also the same ones who end up helping the rest of us attain more than we thought we were capable of.

While they may rise above their fellows, they also bring value to other people's lives at the same time. These individuals should be recognized and acknowledged, if only for this immeasurable value they bring to the culture. For such people have the ability and willingness to breathe life into what is rapidly becoming a dying and dead society. You'll find that the power of the mind's eye is ready when you are.

Law: If you can see it, you can be it.

THE NATURAL BORN SALESMAN

Is there such a person as this? Someone born with a native style that fits the accepted salesperson template offered by conventional wisdom?

Or is the art of selling an acquired skill resulting from disciplined study and practice in the field? Personally, I think it's a little of both, leaning toward the study and practice side.

It's true that some salespeople use only a few of the conventional strengths associated with the profession and still find an acceptable degree of success. But, transplant them to a different sales situation and they will often *come a cropper*, and run into difficulties.

Why? Because they're using one tool, arguably an important one, but still their sales tool kit is somewhat limited. Selling is a human activity and human beings are different one to another. Sometimes you have to adjust your selling style to match theirs.

Unless you, as a salesperson, are able to *adjust your selling techniques to the customer*, you will always lose out to someone who can.

This fact alone *highlights the limitations* of the *natural born* salesperson. This type can sell when the customer fits into what this salesperson is good at. But, being good at only one thing will severely limit your opportunities.

The real secret to success in sales is to *align your selling* techniques to the underlying nat*ural laws of selling*. Now, all that being said, is there such a thing as the natural born salesman? If there is such a person, it is one who has an *inborn ability to connect with people and engender affection and trust*. Combine those native abilities with the basic principles and practiced techniques and you'll have the winning combination every time!

THE PROFESSIONAL BUYER

"**D**on't give me that touchy-feely BS, he said. Just give me your best price. If it works for me, I'm interested, otherwise, don't bother me," he said gruffly.

Have you ever run into this attitude from a prospect?

These types think they know more about your product or service than you do. Of course, sometimes, they do. But often it is just a façade. They're trying to show you that *they are not a pushover.*

Don't confuse this with the real professional buyer. These are the veterans who been through it all before and know exactly what they want. Sometimes, they have a been there - done that type attitude, and take pride in this fact.

At times, it seems like they speak a different language that can be intimidating if you're not prepared for it.

But don't let this throw you.

Professional buyers know that inexperienced salespeople cannot handle the *in your face* type attitude. Often, this is just their way of *separating the wheat from the chafe.* It tells them whether or not it is worth their time dealing with you.

But, you may be surprised that the professional buyer is actually easier and quicker to close on the deal than any other, if you're prepared and know what you're doing.

With this customer type, there is no slow, easy approach to the sale. You'd better know your business, because you could find yourself in a closing situation right off the bat. The worst mistake you can make is to go to the meeting unprepared. This is where *planning, preparation, and practice* set you apart from the competition. Be ready to *think fast, act faster,* and still hit the target. *Information is power* in this situation. Do your research thoroughly. You'll find out *why they buy and what they buy,* in what quantities, at what price and so on. Get all the information you can. This fact alone will *get their attention* and distinguish you from the competition.

Above all, you can't just *wing it.* You're selling hard-hitting facts and figures that end up with a bottom line that they are interested in. If you can do this, you're hitting them where they live.

But at the end of the day, professional purchasing agents are still just people. They respond to the same things all people do in terms of respect, interest, knowledge, skill, and professionalism.

If you are respectful of their time and experience, it will show and you'll be taken seriously.

Preparation and practice will give you the *confidence* you need to handle them every time.

Here are four points to remember when dealing with them:

1. *Prepare.* Do the research until you know their business, competition, and pressure points better than they do.
2. *Show* them you have what they need, before they know it.
3. *Surprise* them. Give them something they didn't expect. Give them a reason to do business with you again.

You'll find a much more receptive audience next time. They're really easier to deal with than you think, once you speak the language.

THE ROUTE TO SALES MASTERY

It's an interesting road to travel once you begin on *the route to sales mastery*; and it's not for the faint of heart. It is filled with challenges beyond the pale, with highs and lows outside the boundaries of the conventional. But if a life of excitement and accomplishment are to be your future, sales mastery is a worthy goal.

Good enough just doesn't cut it anymore. The world has changed and the bar has been raised. You're competing in a global economy these days and if your level of expertise is not moving toward mastery, you're falling behind. The difference between average and mastery is found in how much character, initiative and persistence you bring to the game.

To begin, *the route to sales mastery* requires a sense of humility. We must admit that there are things we don't know, or we are forever stuck with only what we know right now.

The next step is a clear-cut, explicit decision directed toward the attainment of a desirable final result, free from doubt or reservation.

Also *the process* must be as interesting and fulfilling as the result.

If you're unwilling to do the mundane, or practice with great attention on the small detail, mastery will not be forthcoming.

Savor the process; relish the sweat and tears of the process, as they add depth, fullness and flavor to the end result.

If you can hold that deep visceral reaction of living your dream, visualizing how it would affect your life and the lives of others while you are creating it, you're at least half way there.

But, there's a hitch. You live in a world where others have their own dreams, visions and aspirations too, often in competition for the same goals you're after.

The key is: *Who wants it more?*

Do you possess the will to persevere in the fact of failure? Can you pick yourself up and start again, and again? Can you view failure as an opportunity to learn and grow instead of a punishment? If your answer is yes, then the odds of succeeding, though not guaranteed, are in your favor.

Putting your *dreams into action* requires courage, audacity, and boldness, in addition to qualities of initiative, *persistence, and an indefatigable thirst for success. Anything less is not enough unless you wish to be an average, plodding success.*

Ask yourself these questions.

Can you stick to your decision, your vision, even when you run into resistance and opposition?

Can you hold to your dream even when others plant seeds of doubt?

Can you maintain your own point of view even when circumstances seem to dictate that the odds are stacked against you?

The willingness to confront is vital, but the ability to *continue to confront* is equally if not more important.

A major reason few achieve their vision is that they become distracted and dispersed by the noise and clutter of everyday life. In our world where channel-changer mentality is the norm, some wish for instant gratification without effort.

But, in real life, it doesn't work that way.

Winners direct their focus and energies to one overriding target. They possess a kind of inner radar (*some call this luck*) directing them toward opportunity to attainment of their goals. They are constantly on the look-out for a way, not searching for an excuse.

It's the first thing they think about when they wake up and the last when they fall asleep. And they have the self-discipline to concentrate on their goals in spite of every invitation to do otherwise.

The three steps are:

1. *Make a clear, unambiguous decision* of what you intend to accomplish. At that moment the universe begins a process of aligning to your dictates, rather than the reverse, to help bring about the changes you desire.

2. *Hold on to that decision* in all your thoughts and actions no matter what obstacles, barriers or distractions appear to stop you.

3. *See the end result* in your minds eye of what you want to achieve and imagine how that would feel to you.

Most people have no idea of the powerful resources ready to do their bidding once the *decision* is made to really focus on mastering something.

Sadly, they never give the command. Instead, they leave it all to luck or chance and mostly end up on the scrap heap of life. Why not *let the universe adjust to your decisions* and dictates for a change?

Others, already recognized masters in their own fields, agree:

"When you see a thing clearly in your mind, your creative "success mechanism" within you takes over and does the job much better than you could do it by conscious effort or willpower." - Maxwell Maltz

"Obstacles are those frightful things you see when you take your eyes off your goal." - Henry Ford

"Only one who devotes himself to a cause with his whole strength and soul can be a true master." - Albert Einstein.

"First say to yourself what you would be, and then do what you have to do." – Epictetus

"The best day of your life is the one on which you decide your life is your own. No apologies or excuses. No one to lean on, rely on, or blame. The gift is yours - it is an amazing journey - and you alone are responsible for the quality of it. This is the day your life really begins." - Bob Moawad, best selling author

Small goals won't give you the power to overcome the inevitable doubts, fears and distractions you run into along the way. Think big! Now, think bigger.

Ignore the distractions, the doubts, excuses, the worries and reasons why something can't be done, and they'll fall by the wayside like so many insignificant pebbles.

Your future begins with you. Make it what you want.

Law: Your future is going to be remarkably similar to what you are doing right now.

THE SECRET COIN

You can't buy it and you can't sell it. It's more valuable than gold. It's invisible, intangible, and seemingly unattainable unless you're born with it. This secret coin has two sides of equal importance. One side is *credibility* and the other is *expertise*. Each side must be honestly earned for this coin to have any value.

Here's how it works.

Credibility

Credibility is trust. The basis of every successful sales relationship that you develop is trust. The observer accepts what you say as true and believable, or they don't.

The root of the word *credibility* traces back to its Latin origins: *to believe or trust.* It's recognizable to anyone when it's present and uncomfortably obvious when it's not.

Fundamentally, it's a *perception*, formulated by what someone thinks, feels and observes about you. It's detectable yet untouchable, abstract, but obvious at the same time. In short, *you'll know it when you see it.*

When you're selling a service, especially something intangible where there is no concrete evidence that it exists, customers liberally rely on *impressions* to establish a level of trust – something that is difficult to build and easy to destroy.

Trust is invisible and instinctive. When it exists, the manifestations are clearly in evidence. You'll see it when the prospect begins to relax and feel comfortable with you. But it can't be rushed or compelled. Trust must be given *freely* or not at all. It simply can't be forced on anyone.

Once trust is established, confidence will emerge. Confidence is a conscious decision more than it is instinctive. It is built largely on good reasons, definite evidence, or past experience.

Expertise
An expert is an individual who is very knowledgeable, skilled, experienced and able to demonstrate effortless competence *in a certain field.*

Like credibility, expertise is a subjective perception based on opinions and feelings rather than objective facts or evidence. And what you're saying is often less important *than how you're saying it.*

If you can express yourself with clarity, simplicity and humanity to people in a language they can understand and use, you're an expert, at least to them.

Curiously, when everyone agrees that you're an expert – you *are an expert* and you *gain credibility.*

a) As you strengthen your expertise, you increase your credibility.

b) As you increase credibility, you become perceived as an expert.

A credible expert
Being seen as a *credible expert* is an unbeatable combination and increases your value exponentially. It is worth working for.

The secret that makes this coin so important is that these qualities are inextricably intertwined. Each side depends on the other for its value.

When both sides are equally balanced, the intrinsic value is infinite.

This is precisely what every salesperson *needs* – and coincidently – exactly what every customer *wants*.

Chapter 12

THE *START* CHECK

If this concept has been written about in other texts on selling, it has gotten little exposure. This is important material, so read carefully; there are gemstones here.

My son, Evan Jacobs, a successful business executive in his own right, was explaining to me how he was able to always secure funding from the client before he started the job. Getting sufficient payment from the client seemed effortless to him.

What was his secret? Well, the secret is surprisingly obvious and painfully simple. A subtle but powerful change in the way you collect funds at the beginning of the project can make all the difference.

The key change is this: Once they are sold on using your product or service, ask them for a *start check* instead of a *deposit.*

Why? Because *start is an action word* – deposit is *passive* one.

A *start check* is proactive in that it implies immediate action and potential results and benefits. A *deposit check* implies just letting it sit there until they decide how or when to move ahead.

This slight change in wording has the advantage of focusing the attention on the fact that things are going to begin happening on the project the minute that payment is made. As the parting with funds seems antipathetic to human nature in general, this change in the focus of attention makes the process less painful.

Also, this basic principle of providing services is relevant:

Law: The perceived value of any service diminishes once it is delivered.

When the client is under time pressure to get the sales up or make their quarterly targets, they are willing to agree to nearly anything if you can help them accomplish this. However, once you have begun work or have accomplished some of the objectives, the problem seems less significant than it was at the beginning. Your solution now has less perceived value, as the pain has diminished considerably as a result of your work.

Make sure you get the *start check before you begin* and it will be easier on both of you.

If the client wants you to get started on his project, but has reservations as to whether or not he will be able to continue or fund the whole thing, break it into separate areas with each step of the program to be funded when it is initiated.

Get a start check for each program step before you begin any work. They'll get the benefit and you'll get the work.

The client who says, *"We just need you to get started on this now, don't worry, the money will be there,"* is asking you to solve a problem for them that will no longer exist once you start on the project.

It is nearly axiomatic that if they say, "Don't worry about the money;" - *worry about the money.*

Never apologize for asking to have a start check before you begin work. Money and funding has a strange way of disappearing and being used for other more current issues once their immediate problem is handled. The pressure on them is always at its highest before you begin.

The clear message to them should be that once you start on their project, you are directing the *engine* of your company (attention, time and energy) in their direction to solve their problems.

You make commitments, schedule time and personnel, buy supplies for delivery, engage other vendors, creative people, etc. This is part of your "stock in trade" as a company.

Your company resources are being spent at the moment you begin to allocate them in the direction of this client. You have a responsibility to your company to spend these assets in a manner that is consistent with the viability and solvency of your company.

If you spend this resource without securing payment first at some reasonable percentage, you have now wasted something that can never be gotten back.

Time, money, personnel, space, mental energy, creative thought, attention and other costs, all are being spent with nothing in return.

Not exactly a recipe for success in business.

Here are some examples of the correct use of the "start check" concept in use.

Let's say you have what seems to you to be a serious plumbing problem at home on the weekend that you have company coming. You need it handled immediately and it is very important to you. You'll pay almost anything to make this problem go away, now!

The perceived value of a solution is at its highest level. You finally find a plumber who is willing to come out on the weekend and he can be here in an hour. The plumber arrives and you begin to think in terms of the problem being solved – your hopes begin to rise.

Now, if that plumber is wise, he will investigate the problem and before starting to fix anything, will take this next step. He should say, "I can see what the problem is, and I can fix the problem today, but it will cost you $200." What the plumber is really saying is that he knows he should nail down the price first, before he starts. This is his version of the "start check."

He knows that once the problem has been solved, your perception of the value of his service will be far less than it was at the beginning.

Normally, you will pay what he asks without question, as he is seen as the solution to the embarrassment and inconvenience you will experience if the problem remains unhandled.

Also, he is here, now, and says he can make this bad experience all go away. You WANT him to get started and the sooner the better. You'll pay his fee, and happily so.

Isn't it funny how much you will happily pay for an ice-cold bottle of water on a sweltering day at an outside sporting event; a gallon of gas for your empty tank on a deserted off ramp in the middle of the Arizona desert at 1:00AM; a doctor who can give exactly the right diagnosis and prescription for your physical ailment; or the computer tech who solves a problem in 3 minutes that has plagued you for days in preparing that important document.

So, it is your duty and responsibility as a salesperson to close the deal and secure payment at the best possible moment.

Usually that is when the pain of the problem is the highest – *before you start work*. Get that "start check" unless you are certain you have a clear understanding how and when you expect payment.

Using the concept and wording of the *start check* also accomplishes three specific benefits for both the buyer and the seller:

1. The start check buys the "mind share" and creative energy of the one delivering the service or selling the product.

2. Use of this concept takes the attention off the money and puts it where it should be – on the client receiving the benefits of what you have to offer.

3. It has the effect of getting everyone's attention going in the same direction at the same time so the greatest amount of energy can be focused on accomplishing the goal.

So the secret is out. The concept of the *start check* is yours to use as you see fit the minute you understand it.

Now, let's get out there and put it to use. Start!

THE UNREASONABLE MAN

"All progress depends on the unreasonable man, he said firmly." The complete quote from George Bernard Shaw follows:

"The reasonable man adapts himself to the world; the unreasonable one persists in trying to adapt the world to himself. Therefore all progress depends on the unreasonable man."

"Got it?" Said our motivational speaker of the day.

Well, by the end of the short but pithy motivational talk, most of us did get it. I know I did. And not surprisingly, everything Mr. Shaw said hit directly at the heart of all successful selling.

Here's what I took away from his message:

Only the *unreasonable man* – one with sufficient boldness, audacity and courage to put *ideas into action and dreams into reality* – has the chance to change his life and the lives of others.

Such people are able to see a change as something for the better, and set out to make it happen without doubt or uncertainty. Instead of looking for *reasons why they shouldn't expect more*, they search for ways to make it happen.

To them, fairly good, moderately successful, or it's always been that way, just doesn't cut it.

The message really made sense to me because I began to see that *unreasonable* was a good word - one that describes certain people who possess this desirable characteristic.

Change does not occur without a willingness to challenge the mold of tradition, and become more unreasonable and far less *reasonable, (which I began to see is an undesirable characteristic).*

There is no reason I couldn't do anything I set my mind to. I didn't have to accept the excuses, explanations and reasons of why something couldn't be done. The only reason why something didn't get done was because I took my eye off the goal and started looking for reasons why I might fail.

It became clear to me that *looking for reasons to explain failure,* even before I tried, was the "reasonable or logical" way to approach something.

And that only by being *unreasonable* would I find a way to succeed in spite of everything.

This has been said before, but deserves restating:

"If you really want to do something, you'll find a way. If you don't, you'll find an excuse." - Jim Rohn

If progress depends on the unreasonable man, then that is the direction I need and want to go. And unless I miss my guess, *it's the same for you!*

THREE CLASSES OF PEOPLE

There are people who simply do not see what they are looking at; even when it's obvious or pointed out to them, they either refuse or are unable to see it. There are various reasons for this; individual prejudices, preferences, fixed ideas, habits and other influences.

But for our purposes, I believe this quote from Leonardo da Vinci summarizes it best:

"There are three classes of people: those who see. Those who see when they are shown. Those who do not see."

A closer look at this is in order:

1. Those who see.
2. Those who see when they are shown.
3. Those who do not see.

It appears to me that you're wasting your time trying to sell anything to the third class of people. Why? Because *they do not see.*

These people have no foresight and no imagination. They are virtually impossible to sell anything. To them you're speaking a different language, completely outside their reality.

Don't waste your energy as even when they claim to be open to listening to you, they start with a firm attitude of "*I don't know,*" and no matter what you do, they end up with an equally firm, "*I don't know.*"

They remain unaffected by anything you tell or show them. Why should this surprise you? They can't see!

The first two classes, however, can be sold something. The people in class one – *those who can see* – are your easiest to get interested but sometimes your hardest to close. *They can see,* which gives them imagination and vision. But sometimes they are hard to nail down.

They start out wanting what you're presenting but before you know it, they're on to something else, leaving you with no sales-close. Their imagination runs away with both them and your sale.

Those in class two, *those who see when they are shown,* will respond to stories, demonstrations and interaction with your service or product.

Engage them, get them "behind the wheel" so they experience the benefit for themselves and they can be sold with less effort than the other two classes.

To maximize your returns on investment of time and energy, learn to tell the difference between the three classes of people mentioned at the start of this article.

Then pick your battles and you'll end up with much better results with less frustration.

TIMELESS SELLING CONCEPTS

Here are a random list of unchanging selling concepts for you to refer to when all else fails, or even when it doesn't.

All of these are either natural laws in their own right or are based on universal principles of selling.

Keep the customer satisfied – help them get what they want and deliver what you promise.

All things not being equal, people would *still rather* do business with people they like.

Smile and mean it. Don't smile if you don't mean it.

Don't talk about your troubles. Never complain. Never bad-mouth the competition.

Be honest and worthy of trust; never promise what you can't deliver.

When possible, dress like them, talk like them, all the while still being you.

Demonstrate your competence, don't just talk about it.

It's not who you know, *it's who knows you!*

Stop talking before they stop listening.

Are you really interested in what they're saying?

Like and trust yourself first and they'll like and trust you.

Care for the customer through the whole selling process from start to finish and beyond.

Find what you have in common. People like people who like them.

Listen to learn. Learn to lead.

Sell the dream not the product.

People only buy when they see as a benefit.

Logic tells. Stories Sell.

There are three closes in every sale: sales, legal, and the administrative close.

What's important is not how well you talk, but how well you listen.

Personal contact is the best marketing tool you have.

People never forget how you made them feel, for better or for worse.

Sell what they want to buy, not what you need to sell.

If they can't see it, they won't feel it. If they don't feel it, they won't buy it.

Interest, directed by concern or curiosity, attracts attention.

Attention is like a spotlight. Wherever you shine it, tends to attract attention. Keep your attention on them.

Selling is about the people: Understand people and you'll understand selling.

The principles of selling are far more important than the techniques.

Market to people, sell to the individual.

Focus on the natural laws of selling first, then develop your own methods of applying them.

TRUST, BUT VERIFY

A s a rule of thumb, I tend to trust people. But, while I've mostly managed to retain my glass is half-full outlook on life over the years, I've lost a fair amount of innocence and gained a bit more skepticism.

Greater thinkers than I have said that good judgment comes from bad experience, and that most of that comes from bad judgment.

I agree – adding only that the trouble with using experience as a guide, is that *the final exam often comes before the lesson.*

So, how can anyone learn the lessons of life while minimizing the pain and trauma in doing so?

One of the best tools I've found and adopted is the *trust but verify* concept.

It works in dealing with people in sales and business, specifically, but also with people in general. It was good advice when I first heard it and I wish I had taken it to heart at that time. The adage recommends that while someone may be considered reliable, you should also do what you can to verify that his or her information is trustworthy.

By a large percentage, not everyone you run into will have the characteristics described below in this article. But if you do run into one of these characters and don't recognize it, this fact alone can cause *untold trouble* to your life, your family and your career.

The personality trait to which I'm referring, is found in the person who plays *fast and loose with the truth.* Yes, we've all done this on occasion, if only to maintain the social calm and not unnecessarily upset things. But, I'm talking about an individual with a somewhat more sinister attribute: one who is a habitual liar.

Such people lie for no apparent reason. They also count on the basic goodness of the rest of us to get away with dishonesty, deceit and manipulation as a way of life.

It's hard to face that some people could be this way; far easier to dismiss such aberrant behavior, thinking, "It's probably a bad childhood" or "Oh, bless his heart. I'm sure he means well."

But still, to not call them on it – when you have the chance – only allows them to use the same con on others.

How do you know when you're dealing with this character?

There are two distinguishing signs:

1. The first is the big lie - which disguises the truth by making it in-credible – meaning *not credible*, and therefore, not believable.

The *big lie* is far more common than you might think.

"If it sounds too good to be true, it is," is a maxim used to identify such methods.

But I've always thought, the maxim "If it sounds too good to be true, it's likely illegal," also supports this concept perfectly.

2. The second is the *little lie*. This is used to slide in an untruth, unnoticed under the blanket of general truth.

Often the little lie turns out to be the more important than all other factors. "The devil is in the details," is a truism often applied in this circumstance.

In either case, if you can help it, you're better off not doing business with either kind. Once you recognize the methods such people use all the time, you'll never be fooled again, or at least not so often.

Here's my take on this. I've compiled a list of one-liners from my own experience to open your eyes to what these personalities are really up to. Your experiences and opinions may differ from my own, but at least these may give you pause for thought to take a step back and look at what's really going on.

If something *feels wrong*, it is wrong.

Not everyone is a liar, but *anyone can be.*

If they're lying to others, they're lying to you.

If someone is trying to manipulate you, *they're also lying to you.* If they're lying to you, they're trying to manipulate you.

If it sounds *too good to be real,* it's probably *illegal.*

All people lie *some* of the time, some people lie *all* of the time.

People can justify anything. Chronic liars *justify everything.*

Trust your instincts, intuition, and perception or you won't have them for long.

Liars are always looking out for only their own *self-interest*, no matter what they're saying to the contrary.

If you are only hearing *what you want to hear*, *you're being set up.*

All liars are cowards. All cowards will lie.

I sincerely believe your life and career will become smoother and easier to navigate by using this simple tool: *trust, then verify.*

TRUST YOURSELF FIRST

It's a natural law that *trust engenders trust;* but first, you must be honest with, and *trust yourself.*

Now, we've all had our trust betrayed by slick con-men in the form of banksters, lawyers, politicians, and other thieves many times.

So many times, in fact, that it's no surprise we're slow to trust anyone anymore. Sadly, this is particularly true in the business of sales.

You must recognize that **trust factor** (the lack of) is a major barrier to all sales. It is something you cannot neglect or ignore and still expect to survive in this profession.

The element of trust between you and the prospect deserves your full attention before anything else. Don't try to brush it off and hurriedly try to get into the sales presentation. If you do, you're wasting your time and the attention of the customer.

Trust is a personal consideration. People rely on instincts, impressions and other tiny signals to tell if you're worthy of their trust or if they should remain skeptical or suspicious.

Just because you say the words, *trust me,* doesn't mean they have to or will.

Trust is the glue that holds it all together; it's something that weaves its way through every step in the sales cycle.

If handled perfectly, the final close is as natural as rain and easy to accomplish. But drop the ball on the *trust factor* at any step along the way and it's like pulling teeth without an anesthetic. Following is a look at the trust factor in relationship to the five-step sales cycle.

Contact

The contact with an individual (not a job title) often comes from a personal referral, which along with personal contact is the best way to start building trust.

If a genuine friend says you're trustworthy, they'll give you the benefit of the doubt. At least *until you prove them wrong.* You can't buy trust, but you can earn it. As you have only one chance to make a first impression, you must make it a good one. Time spent on preparation, planning and drilling your introduction will pay large dividends as you move forward.

Qualification

The second step is qualification. Most sales reps think the qualification step is where you determine if the prospect is qualified to purchase what they are selling. But this is a double-edged sword and *it cuts both ways.*

The qualification step is also *when the prospect is qualifying you!*

The prospect is thinking: Do you have a verifiable track record? Are you credible? Are you trustworthy? What are your values? Are you straightforward and easy to understand? How does it feel to be around you?

The prospect is establishing a position in their mind of you, your company, and your service or product. Once this position is formed, for better or for worse, it's not easy to change.

Presentation

No matter what form this may take, it is essentially the point when you *show your goods.*

When you reach this point, the stage should be set for you to make your presentation.

Trust is also an important element at this point as well. The prospect trusts you with their attention, their time, and their interest. But, stray off the point, waste their time and attention by sending mixed messages and you'll lose them quickly.

You're the expert, *don't just tell them; show them.*

They are putting their trust in you to take them on a path of increasing awareness of the personal **benefit to them** that your product or service will be.

At this point, they are still hoping that you'll show them something. This is your chance. Use it or lose it.

If you have misrepresented yourself in any way, you'll break the bond of trust, usually permanently.

Handling Objections

In a typical sales cycle, the next step is handling objections. The salesperson, by this time, has determined the customer's priorities and will be explaining the benefits and downplaying the negatives of what seems to be the best fit based on the first three steps as above.

Most sales people know that a disinterested client doesn't come up with objections. Only a client who is *interested* in what you're offering brings up objections.

You must handle these in a way to **maintain the trust** that you've built up already between you and the prospect. This is where they discover more about you.

Do you maintain your interest in them? Are you still as polite as you were in the beginning? Or do you dismiss their concerns as unimportant or brush them aside as insignificant? How you handle (or don't handle) objections relate directly to them continuing to trust you or not. Careful listening and skillful, interested handling of their concerns and worries will win the day in handling objections.

The Close

The closing step gets a bad reputation only when you skip the vital steps leading up to it.

This step is **when the trust factor is truly tested**. The subject of money (always a hot topic) has to come into the equation at some point. You can't avoid it.

But, it is very common for *previous betrayals* on the subject of money to come flooding back to mind, almost unconsciously.

But, if you've done the prior steps completely, this step is quite matter of fact and is easily accomplished. If you can handle this step without personal tension, anxiety or stress of any kind, this alone can calm the fears of the prospect.

When you demonstrate a calm, confident (and truthful) manner in dealing with this step, it makes it easier for everyone.

Commonly it's only necessary to tell them the price, arrange for payment and find out when they want to start.

If you've done each step to good result, the close is just like taking the final step up a stairway.

It's easy and natural. It also proves to the prospect that *they were right in trusting you* from the beginning!

UNANSWERED COMMUNICATION

Okay, I've go to get something off my chest. I find it maddening how some people rarely respond to anything. And even if they do grace you with an answer, it seems automated – like the *gotcha* type answer, as if they never glanced at the mail or listened to the message you sent them.

So, what's up with this anyway?

With more forms of communication available to us than at any time in history it seems like the *unanswered communication* wouldn't be a problem. But it is, and it's getting worse. As expert communication skills are the *core competency* of anyone involved in selling, these skills form the basis from which you operate in getting the job done, no matter what *method* of selling is required.

The unanswered communication is a symptom that something is wrong with these skills. Salespeople and prospects alike seem to think that a communication is complete when they've read or heard what was sent and that it requires nothing further from them. Further, the acknowledgements that issue from some people are often as unsatisfying as they are inadequate.

It's my experience that any unanswered communication leaves your attention stuck to some degree, wondering if they even got your message. It acts like a mental post-it note in your mind reminding you that the communication is still incomplete. Eventually becoming a **hidden attention magnet** that grabs even more attention every time you think about it.

The punch line is that the unanswered communication is only a **symptom** of a larger and far more serious problem. Every salesperson knows – or should know – that communication is the exchange of information between people resulting in a sense of mutual understanding and shared agreement.

An acknowledgment is some sign or indication showing that you've been heard, a response that indicates you're sensing, feeling or seeing the same thing at the same time.

It could be sometime as subtle as a knowing nod, a smile, and a pat on the back, anything that lets the other person know he or she exists and has been heard. When you fail to acknowledge someone's origination to you, you also send the message that they are not important enough to deserve a response.

And, of course, sending the message that you don't care about a customer can ruin your chances of a long-term relationship. After all, you're in the business of making friends and creating sales, aren't you?

All this requires is a sincere **interest in and caring about** the customer, and whether or not you respond to what they say speaks volumes about how much you care about them - for better or for worse.

UNIVERSAL SELLING PRINCIPLES

Universal selling principles are common sense, time-tested laws. They are self-evident, inviolable truths; natural laws which underlie all selling activities.

Knowledge of the correct principles will give you an understanding of how people work and why they do the things they do and once you understand people; you'll understand all selling. Stephen Covey agrees with this concept, when he says:

"I believe that correct *principles are natural laws*, we need great courage to lead our lives by correct principles and to have integrity in the moment of choice."

The correct principles have three primary characteristics:

1. They are obvious
2. They are simple
3. They work

I can guarantee you one thing: If you're having trouble with your selling procedure or sales closing techniques, or your life, the *correct principles are not to blame.*

The source of the trouble is that the basic principles are not being applied correctly.

This is an observation that can be easily seen by anyone who cares to look: It is absolutely imperative that you know, understand and apply each of these principles if your goal to succeed in sales, or live life.

Why? Because when your methods or tactics don't line up with your principles you're *setting yourself up for trouble*. People who should know better make this mistake every day.

So, why do some continue to disobey these universal laws of selling? Here's the answer:

Nearly all trouble comes from an *ignorance* of the fundamental principles of selling, not from the methods being used.

Changing, willy-nilly, your methods of selling, is like putting your trust in luck to correct the problem. It's a crapshoot that doesn't work.

Only the essential, time-proven basic selling principles will right the ship and fill the sails with wind again.

Absent these guiding principles as your rudder, inevitably you will find yourself (at best) adrift in sea of confusion; or afloat with the flotsam and jetsam remaining after a shipwreck at sea (at worst).

These are the axiomatic rudiments – indispensable to success in selling, and they provide the tools to build a stable, secure, foundation that can launch your progress into the big leagues.

They can withstand the confusions and difficulties that go with and day-to-day selling activities because they are based on *common sense basics* available to everyone.

And they not some *newest and latest* sales fad that changes faster than you can say *"spit."*

Stability, predictability and prosperity are the result of knowing and practicing correctly the natural laws of selling.

WHAT ARE YOU DOING *RIGHT*?

Here are 25 basic ideas that form the bedrock of all selling activities that you must be familiar with.

You don't need to know all of them to get started, as a careful study of just a few of them will shore up your confidence.

If you're already familiar with some of the principles, a quick review will affirm the reasons for your success and provide a foundation for building an even more successful career.

Note: A short answer follows each question.

25 Basic Selling Principles

1. 1What is the basic purpose of sales or selling? (To bring about a willing exchange between two or more people for mutual benefit)

2. What is the working definition of sales? (To help the prospect achieve a purpose they once had, one they have now, or want to set up for the future)

3. What is the action definition of all selling? (The effective use of communication to cause an increase in desire, enhance the value of a product or service in the eyes of the customer resulting in a willing exchange of something of value for the thing wanted or needed to the benefit of both parties)

4. What is the most important thing to establish *before you start* the selling process? (Establish the personal purposes of the salesperson)

5. What is the most effective way to get the prospect or customer to trust you? (*Trust yourself first*)

6. What is the easiest way to get someone interested in you? (Get interested in them and contact the individual not the job title)

7. 7What is the best way to get someone's attention? (Tell a story and surprise them)

8. How do you know when the other person is ready to listen to what you have to say? (They start being interested in you and asks questions)

9. What are two things that will squelch any deal? (Uncertainty and doubt)

10. What type of person is almost impossible to sell to? (Someone with no imagination)

11. What is the best way to ruin your selling future? (Blame the customer)

12. What do customers remember least about your presentation? (What you say)

13. What do clients *never forget* about your presentation? (How you made them feel)

14. What is the surest way to create sales resistance? (Forcing the customer)

15. How can you get the client to reach for you? (Ask a question about something relevant to their problem, then withdraw slightly)

16. What is the simplest way to defuse an objection or an argument? (Listen, clarify and make sure it's not a red herring. Once you isolate the real problem, find out how important it is and how you can help them get what they want)

17. What is the time-tested way to close any deal? (Remind them of their purposes and how you can help them achieve it)

18. What do you do if they are fixed on one problem that *can't be solved*? (It's either the wrong problem, or it's the wrong solution. Find out which and handle)

19. What if the prospect can't make a decision? (There is something they don't understand or you skipped a step in the sales process)

20. What if the client is stuck on an old solution that doesn't work anymore? (It is a solution to some earlier confusion; address the earlier confusion)

21. What are the three post-closing steps that must occur for the deal to stay closed? (The sales close; the legal close; and the administrative close)

22. What do you do when they say it costs too much? (Don't argue with them. Instead, acknowledge and then ask them: "How much too much is it? What were they prepared to pay for it?" Remember, they never expected to get it for nothing)

23. What is the best way to handle any complaint? (Use the "feel, felt, found" principle. For example, "I know how you feel and others have felt the same way. But we found after looking carefully at the details, it really was the right choice)

24. What are the easiest steps to sell anything? (Tell them a story; show them and let them experience it). Once you have obtained all the information necessary for a perfect presentation that addresses their purposes and needs, ask one of the three easy questions to close the deal: #1 "Have we covered all the points you were interested in?" #2. "Does the program make sense to you?" #3."When would you like to start?"

25. What is the easiest way to lose a sale? (Fail to ask for the order)

There are many more principles and methods to learn and practice to become a sales master. But these twenty-five basic principles alone can rapid-launch your career and strengthen what *you have been doing right* all along.

WHAT ARE YOU THINKING?

Words of wisdom from Ralph Waldo Emerson:

"A man is what he thinks about all day long."

And, in my opinion, he was right. Unfortunately, however, the reverse is also true: **What you think about all day long, you become.**

This is a powerful, fundamental principle with enormous potential to help you to succeed in life. But, like any power-tool, you have to know how to use it. To illustrate, here is an old story of how the sea became salty.

A thief stole the king's magical millstone; able to produce anything that was wished for. After a successful getaway by boat, he felt hungry.

His bread was, however, a tad too sweet, so he tapped the millstone and wished for some salt.

Unfortunately, he had no clue how to stop it, so it kept on churning salt, until the boat sank, and the millstone with it, to the bottom of the sea, where it still lies to this day, pouring out salt.

The thief in the story had a powerful tool, with the capability of doing anything he wanted, but he didn't know how to use it. Similarly, *your mind is the most powerful tool* you possess and it works in very much the same way.

It is like to a powerful, perpetual-motion copy machine with unique capabilities.

It is always on; ready to do your bidding at a moments notice; capable of multiplying copies of everything you think about, and do it endlessly. Further, it never wears out and never stops. In fact the more it's used, the stronger it becomes.

This is how you end up becoming what you think about most. What your attention is on influences your thoughts. What you're thinking about tends to activate your emotions. What you're feeling arouses and stimulates your actions.

WHAT BUSINESS ARE YOU IN?

"**O**kay, *what business are you in, really?*" the speaker asked, with just the hint of a smile in her voice. Her response to my nearly inaudible answer took me completely by surprise, just as she expected it would.

She continued, "The undeniable truth is that you're in the people business, handling the individual. Everything else is secondary."

A bit thrown off my game, I still managed a feeble reply. *"Umm, I see where you're going, but . . ."*

She interrupted, "If your attention is not on the people, you're focused on the wrong target."

And you know what, she was right! You're not in the sales business, marketing business, computer business, or any other business if you ignore the *people*. Because, if the *human factor* is left out of the equation, there won't be any business at all.

As much as we like to talk about technology, processes, ideas, and systems, no matter what line of business you're in, one thing remains unshakably true:

Many highly successful people, from very diverse walks of life, agree.

For example, Doyle Brunson, celebrated professional poker player, gave his personal insight into his consistent, unfailing success over many decades. "To win as a professional, you must realize that you're in the people business – while you're playing cards. **The more you know about people, the better your chances of winning.**"

Herb Pomeroy, renowned educator and trumpeter of Berkeley College of Music, and widely recognized as the "musician's musician," had his own version of the same concept. "In my early professional years, I thought music was the most important thing. I came to realize that I was wrong. **The people are the most important thing.**"

Another memorable quote, revealing his underlying philosophy of passion and integrity, attributed to Howard Schultz, Founder and CEO of Starbucks says it this way: **"We are not in the coffee business, serving people, but in the people business, serving coffee."**

It's axiomatic in the game of selling: you're always in the business of *handling the individual.*

The subtle yet profound wisdom and broad implications of this concept cuts to the core of all selling. You can't divorce yourself from this truth and hope to succeed over the long run. Being in the *people business* means that everything you can do to nurture, care for, or help others get along better in life will inevitably end up helping you as well.

Recognizing and applying this, as one of the *natural laws of selling,* is as close as you can get to a guarantee of success. If you're looking for something to *hang your hat on*, something you can believe in and depend on, this is it.

Using this principle will focus your thoughts, clarify your purposes, and simplify your actions and efforts, all in the direction of taking care of business where it really matters. Selling is about people generally, and handling the individual specifically.

WHAT DO YOU EXPECT?

The difference between upscale planning and downscale wishful thinking is this: Some people really do expect to win, and are surprised when they don't.

This expectation permeates their thoughts, their emotions and their body, to prepare them to do whatever is necessary to win. They see themselves having already attained the desired result.

They don't engage in needless worry about it, or sabotage their project by injecting self-doubt of their own abilities before they have even begun.

Importantly, they recognize when others infect and negate the project with their own limitations on what can be done, and take effective steps to handle this.

Question: Why is it that the easiest time to make a sale is right after you have completed a successful sale?

Answer: Because your winning attitude at that instant radiates infectious confidence, certainty and inner pride at having demonstrated your competence.

This is how the **winners think all the time.** They really do expect to win (and include others in their success). Their complete attention is on the accomplishment of the stated goal or target to a successful result.

Their level of expectancy is that things are going to work out as they intended, and they are willing to back it up with whatever effort (backbone) is necessary to make it happen.

Their focus is on the product while enjoying the process.

Expectations are a consequence of three factors:

a) Your attention, b) Your thoughts, c) Your feelings.

All three of these elements must be in agreement with each other to produce the greatest results. Any misalignment will reduce the effectiveness. In this way, what you expect and believe to be true is attracted to you.

Expecting to win can shift the way you see yourself and how others perceive you. It can change your attitude, your body posture, and your view of life.

Why not expect to win? What have you got to lose?

WHAT YOU SHOULD BE SELLING?

Every master salesperson knows that they're not just selling products or services.

They also know you give people something that touches them, not just something they can touch.

Is it really just this simple? Yes, it is when you're operating at the top of the game.

But there is no reason that you can't start using it right now, no matter where you are on the path to becoming a master in salesmanship.

The art of selling: This path, to master the art and craft of selling, starts and ends with *how you make them feel.* Customer decisions are often based on *very small details* in the experience of buying.

These include countless invisible marketing messages: the way someone answers the phone, how they feel upon entering the establishment, how they are greeted, their impressions in the personal interface with the salesperson, how their questions are answered and many more visible and invisible factors.

Each of these elements either contributes to, or negates the buying decisions of the customer.

You must be very clear about what you're selling before you make the first phone call or meet the customer in person. You're always selling a feeling – you're selling an experience, something that moves them and touches them personally.

The senses: The senses are methods by which people become aware of things. The first time you touch a hot stove – you feel pain.

You are now more aware than just a second before it happened. People eventually learn to desire pleasure and avoid painful experiences. Mostly they want more pleasure and less pain.

And what people **feel** is an even deeper and far more powerful sensation. How you make them feel is something they never forget.

How does this affect you as a salesperson? Simple. The title of a hit song by Simon and Garfunkel answers this question perfectly: "*Keep The Customer Satisfied.*"

They want to experience a pleasurable dinner not a rude hostess and careless waiter. They desire a new car that makes them feel successful and important, not something they are ashamed of and have to hide.

It's human nature: People want what is pleasurable and avoid what is painful. *You're selling the hope* that they can have what they want.

People buy the wish for a better life or of attaining a personal goal that has been burning inside for a lifetime. *This is why people buy.* They buy to achieve their own purposes.

What you're selling should be something that will let them experience what it feels like to see their goals as attainable and coming into being.

This is what people want to buy – and exactly what you should be selling.

WHAT YOU THINK, YOU BECOME

Selling is a tough business. Land mines and pitfalls line the narrow path and bar the way to success. One misstep can often lead to disaster in the business world today. So, how do you survive in this somewhat dangerous environment? A look back in history reveals a workable answer that can put you in the driver's seat.

2500 years ago, Gautama Siddhartha said,

"What you think, you become."

His words may be as germane today as they were when uttered, perhaps even more. They have echoed down the centuries, creating a positive influence in everyone who heard and applied them. With just five words Siddhartha outlined a way of living that puts you *in control of your life.* Why? Because your thoughts really do have an effect on your life.

You really can influence your own destiny and create your own future. It all starts with what you're thinking about today.

Whatever opinions and beliefs you may hold on the philosophical efficacy of this concept, the facts are undeniable:

Law: Thoughts influence emotions – and emotions stimulate actions.

Thinking about what you want to achieve, dreaming about possibilities, imagining life the way you'd like it to be and feeling yourself living it can bring about some amazing changes. Some even believe that doing so actually has an impact on the way molecules arrange themselves.

Whether or not you agree, it can't hurt to wake up every morning thinking about your aspirations and believing you can make them happen. No matter what your dreams are, seeing yourself as *having already accomplished your goal* is a powerful technique, based upon an even more powerful principle.

Law: You tend to create what you keep your attention on.

Stephen Covey agrees: "We will be truly effective only when we begin with the end in mind."

You create your our own life and it all starts with your thoughts. A desirable future will be there if you create it today. It all starts with intentionally directing your thoughts and emotions toward what you desire. Even Henry Ford agrees when he said,

"Whether you think you can, or you think you can't, you're usually right."

And as a salesman or woman, the way you feel about yourself has an enormous influence on how others feel about you. Why not start off the day with your thoughts aligned with what you really want?

WHEN IS A SOLUTION NOT ONE?

Here's something that will help you get back on top of your game – in sales or in life.

Question: When is a solution not a solution?

Answer: When it ignores, neglects, explains away or justifies what caused the problem in the first place.

Any solution, which neglects what really caused the problem, isn't one. Desperate moves and bad advice only mask the underlying situation. In fact, they allow the problem to fester and grow more deadly.

A well-known fact is that a *false diagnosis* is worse than none at all, especially when the remedy kills the patient. It's an endless pit and just digging harder won't get you out.

Here is a gemstone I've discovered about solutions in general:

Law: The right solution will never solve the wrong problem. The wrong solution will not solve the right problem.

To have any hope of solving the problem - you must find *the right solution to the right problem.* Some are disinclined to accept this idea, preferring instead to *assume they know the solution* before they understand the problem. But, as Malcolm Forbes suggests,

"It's so much easier to suggest solutions when you don't know too much about the problem."

I agree.

It has been my experience that most people would rather spend energy looking for a solution than confronting the problem. In fact, many of the thorny problems of today had their beginnings as a quick fix to yesterday's problems.

But, sooner or later that *can that we kicked down the road,* ends up at your own doorstep demanding your attention.

Instead of adopting a temporary solution that, all too often, ends up as *permanent problem,* better to resolve to make it a habit of looking directly at the problem when it shows up. Then work out a solution that dissolves it completely. And remember this when someday you find yourself furiously trying to unravel some intractable problem:

Law: An *unsolvable* problem means it's the wrong solution or the *wrong problem.*

Chapter 13

WHO ARE YOU SELLING TO?

You're not selling to yourself are you? I didn't think so. The person (customer) you're selling to is always some other person than yourself.

So, why do so many salespeople think *they have to do all the talking*, all the time?

Are you trying to *impress yourself* about how much you know about your product or service? Or convince yourself that you sound like you know what you're talking about?

As we all know, communication is the key ingredient of ANY type of selling. And the art of listening to the customer is infinitely more important than how much or how fast you can rattle off everything you know.

So, who are you selling to? It's obvious. You're always selling to one person at a time; *the individual in front of you.*

It doesn't matter how simple or complex your sales process, your only job is to sell to the person in front of you, right now.

Focus on the right target and you'll intensify your message. Only sell to one person at a time – the one individual right in front of you, right now. When you convey that they are important, you become more important to them.

Finally this law states it clearly:

Law: You will understand selling once you realize that customers are not there to *solve your problems*, they are looking for a *solution to their problems*.

WHO IS RUNNING THE SHOW?

In just fifteen words, 19th century novelist George Elliot says it all: *"It is never too late to be the person you were always meant to be."*

Read this quote again, and carefully. Digest it word for word, because it applies directly to you as a salesperson.

Known by her pen name, *George Elliot*, she was born Mary Anne Evans in 1819. She went on to become an acclaimed English novelist, one of the leading writers of the Victorian Era.

Her novels are recognized for their realism and psychological insight and the quote above is no exception. And now, inspired by her writing, here are some of my personal thoughts that may find universal applicability.

My personal observations for your edification:

I am not comfortable in my own skin when I *pretend* to be a victim, a slave or to be weaker than I know I am.

I know that **I'm running my own show** and that I'm responsible for whatever situation I am in.

I have a high certainty that the decision, *not to be,* isn't even in the running as an option.

There is only one workable decision. That is: *to be* – because being robotically or hypnotically motivated only by someone else's dictates, desires, or demands on my time and attention equates to no life at all.

The "*re-cognition*" is: I want to be . . . and I want to be me. It's who I really am, anyway, so it's as simple as it is powerful. And, I believe it's the same for you.

The only way you can know what you really want, or do what you want, is to *be who you really are*.

It is impossible to achieve what you really want while living someone else's dreams. You must be who you are meant to be . . . and who you really are. Only then will you get what you want to have.

By the way, an important side-note: Good luck cannot find you if you're not being yourself.

Once unfettered by limitations of pretended powerlessness; free of self-generated considerations of self-abnegation and self-denial; stripped of the limitations of pretentious social veneer – all that remains is what is really important . . . who you really are.

As a salesperson, as long as you are being yourself – no artificial façades, actively involved in life, following your goals, making your own decisions and choices, running your life according to your own dictates and desires – you have a chance to make it what you've always wanted. Riches of insight and awareness, of friendships and relationships, a wealth of expansion, wisdom and prosperity are waiting for you once you wake up and remember this: *You are the one in charge of running your own life.*

WISHBONE OR BACKBONE?

If you've ever felt you have got too much wishbone and too little backbone, this article is for you. Here are some ideas to help you start using your backbone to full capacity.

To accomplish a goal, first you must *give it a name*.

Write it out in brief, clear, unambiguous language. If you are uncertain about what you really are going for, what makes you think you will end up with anything but a vague end result?

Next you have to *decide how much you really want it*. What are you willing to give up or sacrifice to obtain what you want? Wanting implies that it has a desired value or benefit.

Finally, you have to *do whatever is necessary to get it*. Don't look for excuses why something can't be done; look for reasons why it can be.

You can name it and want it, but in this universe, you have to have enough push-through to get it done. You will run into obstacles of all kinds to be sure. Can you continue in spite of all these things, or are you going to give up at the first bump in the road?

Now, to ensure you have enough backbone suitable for any challenge requires three things:

Persistence
Carry out what you have decided upon. The temporary discomfort of self-discipline is far less than the pain of regret. Persistence is your greatest asset. Get 'er done!

Character
If you don't stand for something, you'll stand for nothing. Be honest with yourself. Your character is not the same as your reputation.

Character is who you really are when no one is looking. Reputation is *just what others think you are.*

Commitment
Ignore the distractions; focus on the target. Commitment is what separates those with wishbone from those with backbone. Don't let anything stop you.

But wait - there is one more important element that makes it all work together. Entertainer, Reba McEntire, said it this way,

"To succeed in life, you need three things: a wishbone, a backbone and a funny bone."

I agree. The *wishbone* stimulates imagination, dreams and goals to strive for. The *backbone* is will and determination, which stimulates persistence and courage. But the *funny bone* may well be the most important element of the three.

Your sense of humor allows you to not take life too seriously. And anything you can find humor in, you can survive.

If failure, setbacks and disappointment are the disease, laughter is the cure. Laughter is the relief valve for stresses of life; the rejuvenating force which invigorates your energy and revitalizes your goals.

Keep your sense of humor alive and active. It helps your willingness to persist in spite of anything. It draws your dreams closer and makes them more real; and it makes life worth living for all of us.

This quote by Andrew Carnegie, an enormously successful businessman who raised himself from rags to riches in the steel business, summarizes the concept perfectly: *"There is little success where there is little laughter."*

YOU CAN'T BUY TRUST

I believe we can all agree that all things being equal, people would rather deal with someone they trust. *So, how do we get to the point of trusting anyone?*

Well, we all use our senses constantly to get information about people, the environment and situations. The same is true of trust.

When you are talking to a customer on the phone the invisible sense messages from your words, inflections, tone of voice, enthusiasm, interest (or the lack of) all add up to the listener developing a feeling about you and your company and whether you feel or seem trustworthy or not.

You want to build certain elements such as *trustworthiness*, truthfulness, interest, helpfulness, certainty, confidence and professionalism with every interaction with your public.

But the most important one by far, is trust as this quote from the movie, *Godfather II*, (said by Frank Pentangeli to Michael Corleone) aptly illustrates:

"Your father did business with Hyman Roth, your father respected Hyman Roth, but your father never trusted Hyman Roth."

If they have no other choice, people will do business with you and respect you, but will not necessarily trust you. By definition, trust is either given freely or it isn't trust.

Trust is a word that implies confidence that they can depend or rely on you for something in the future, even if it is a split second from now, it is still considered the future.

You can't buy trust, but over time you may be able to earn it.

With regard to customers and clients specifically, trust is earned by consistently delivering what you promised, when you promised it, time and time again.

Trust is created by a combination of what people hear, what they feel and what they sense intuitively. And it can happen instantly, from the first hello.

They can tell if they can rely on you to care for them and their interests or if you're only trying to sell them something to make a fast buck.

A company is made up of individuals and individuals make up the company. When a customer calls the company, who do they talk to? In spite of the proliferation of automated voice prompts, eventually they get to a live person. And that person could be you.

Their trust in the company begins and ends with you.

If they feel they like you and can trust you, the company is good. If not, then the company is bad.

Every customer expects and deserves to be treated like an individual, not just a body, walking around with a dollar sign stamped on it.

When I walk into a store, sometimes I feel like I have tripped some hidden beam that activates this circuit and this voice out of nowhere blurts out, "*Can I help you?*" Or, when I'm checking out, "*Did you find everything you were looking for?*"

All this is said without any sense of live communication being established. It's just a trained robotic-like statement that some consultant was paid to tell them to memorize. To me, this is more irritating than if they had said nothing. That delicate, initial line of trust with the customer is easily snapped though carelessness, which then requires a deft handling to repair it.

Every interface that a customer has with anyone in the company, whether in person, on the phone, in writing, internet websites, email, marketing of any kind, each and every one of these connections are a vital form of *invisible marketing* of your company, building trust or destroying it.

Whether they can trust you to care for them or not is evident in every *action or inaction* you take. Each of these creates an indelible impression of you and your company. In short, are you are worthy of trust, or not?

Addendum: As trust is often inextricably intertwined with money, I've included 10 quotes from my own experiences on the subject for your amusement, enlightenment, and/or edification:

Never be the lender of last resort, as you will also be the *last to be repaid.*

If your friends see you as an easy touch for a loan, you will soon have an abundance of debtors and a *scarcity of friends.*

The memory of giving a gift of money lasts longer for the *giver* than he who *receives it.*

Trusting a friend with your money is the best way *to lose both.*

Some people - when they don't have a pot to piss in or a window to throw it out of - will manage to find you, no matter how distant or remote. Help them back on their feet again, and they can't remember your name, (but perhaps you should help them anyway).

Only a fool accepts, unquestionably and unconditionally, these words, "Trust me, I'll never let you down." They can, and *often will.*

When they say, "Don't worry about the money" – *worry about the money.*

Borrow money from your children. It's the best way to teach them the value of money.

The key to credibility is to be worthy of trust. The way to inspire trust from others is to first trust you.

Trust is a fragile thing and requires as much care as any other fragile and precious thing. Easy to break, almost impossible to restore.

YOU CAN'T ALWAYS GET WHAT YOU WANT –
or can you?

Sometimes sales wisdom is found in unexpected places, as suggested in the title from the lyrics of a "Rolling Stones" hit song from 1969.

The words of the title underscore two important concepts, basic to all sales: People will find a way to get what they need or want; but they would always rather have both.

So, if you can find a way to let them have both what they want and what they need, it will be the easiest sale you ever make. To accomplish this, it helps to know *why people buy*, not just what they buy.

Of course, the simple answer is that people buy what they need and/or what they want. This is the age-old "needs and wants" theory and it does have workability.

But to take a closer look, why do people buy anything, really? What are the motivating urges that drive them to want or need to have something?

It can be stated with confidence that people buy to escape, lessen or avoid things that cause painful experiences, whether physical, emotional, mental or spiritual; or to satisfy impulses toward securing pleasures of various kinds, such as comfort, health, love and desirable things and conditions in life.

One well-known theory of motivation comes from the *"Hierarchy of Needs Model"* by Abraham Maslow. Briefly, he describes human needs/ wants and motivations as ordered in a pyramid of five levels. Each is a pressing *need, demand or want* that must be mostly satisfied before any attention could be given to the next higher level.

It is widely argued that these factors underlie everything that stimulates, motivates or triggers *the buying impulse.* Prospects are seeking to get what they need, *and if possible,* also what they want - which supports my first contention above.

But human beings and situations in life are not always predictable. Sometimes, people are driven more by their needs, other times more by what they want.

The job of the salesman is to be alert enough to show them *how they can have both.*

Here's how you do it: The more *needs* you can identify, the more they'll *want* what you're offering.

Once the prospect sees that what you are offering is what they *need and want,* the sale is virtually closed. For example, they want to buy a home for the emotional feeling it gives them but tell themselves they need the home as a good investment.

If what you're selling satisfies both objectives, they tend to close the deal themselves.

Give them what they *need and want.* The reason this works is because needs and wants are subjective concepts, which dictate objective satisfaction. When people believe they really *need* something, it is perceived as more *valuable to them and they want it!*

This provides the greatest motivation to buy anything, and they will do nearly anything to get it. It becomes their *raison d'être* at that moment in time.

If what you're selling will help them satisfy both needs and wants you'll have a happy customer and a closed deal, which is also what you need and want.

WHAT YOU EXPECT, YOU PROJECT

Did you know that what you *expect to have happen* could have an enormous effect on the ultimate success or failure of your presentation?

This is because, whether you know it or not, you're sending out *invisible mini-signals* that convey your internal emotions and attitudes to others. These are called micro-expressions and are something you should know about, for they can break a deal and leave you without a clue as to why it happened.

Extensive study and research on the subject of *micro-expressions* conducted by Paul Ekman, Ph.D., has conclusively demonstrated that there are brief, involuntary facial expressions observable in people, indicating an involuntary emotional reaction or attitude.

Commonly this happens when people have something to hide or something to lose or gain, but they can also occur in moments of surprise or strong interest. In any case, such tiny emotional signals are nearly impossible to hide and very easy to miss, because they occur literally in the blink of an eye.

Some professions are trained to recognize mini-signals, such as police or border guards, and they can sense things that the untrained would never see. And as most of us know, wives and mothers all seem to have an uncanny ability to *hear what isn't being said and see what isn't there.*

My wife is one of them; she picks up things all the time that others simply are not even aware of. I believe it's partly instinctive and partly due to these mini-signals that she sees, hears or feels, consciously or unconsciously.

This is invaluable information for any salesperson. For you may be *unknowingly creating negative reactions* in the prospect.

When you have internal insecurities, doubts and anxieties, customers can sometimes feel the same things but misidentify where these feelings are coming from.

Instead they internalize the feeling and begin to doubt themselves, *for no reason.*

As it all happens on an emotional level, logic or explanations will not change how they feel when they *just want to wait and think it over.*

It is a problem because, as you know, *uncertainty and indecision* (in the prospect or the salesperson) can kill a deal faster than anything.

But, these micro-expressions can also work in your favor. Approaching a client, in person or on the phone, with a calm, confident and interested attitude with no attention on yourself, can change your tone of voice, your body language, and the general atmosphere that you project.

This conveys a friendly attitude of interest in the client that can work miracles in influencing the outcome of the meeting.

The old saying, "the best time to make a sales call is just after you've closed a deal" is an example. You're projecting an *atmosphere of winning* that is conducive for creating another close.

The key is to remain *sincerely interested* in understanding and helping the customer at all times. Two things happen when you do this.

Your attention is no longer on your internal insecurities and you'll be in a position to observe these micro-expressions in the customer; which can benefit both of you. Make sure what you're expecting is in line with what you want, because *what you expect - you project.*

YOUR ATTITUDE IS SHOWING

I feel we all need a gentle reminder from time to time of the *importance of attitude*, particularly in the sales profession. It is a profession that requires that you project an upbeat, winning attitude no matter what you're feeling internally.

Your attitude (*mental, physical or spiritual*) is one of the most visible things that you present to others at every interface. Happily this is something that you can control and use to your advantage. Simply being interested in people, the environment, and the world around you (outside your head) gets you in the game and gives you a competitive advantage.

When you project an attitude of *positivity* or *negativity* in everything you say and how you say it –that's what you leave behind after the call or personal meeting.

This quote on the subject, by Charles Swindoll, author, educator, is excellent.

"I believe the single most significant decision I can make on a day-to-day basis is my choice of *attitude*. It is more important than my past, my education, my bankroll, my successes or failures, fame or pain, what other people think of me or say about me, my circumstances, or my position.

Attitude keeps me going or cripples my progress. It alone fuels my fire or assaults my hope. When my attitudes are right, there is no barrier too high, no valley too deep, no dream too extreme, no challenge too great for me."

Your attitude really is showing – *all the time*, for better or for worse. Make sure it's the message you want to convey and is working for you not against you.

YOUR TWO GREATEST ALLIES

There are two elements that you must befriend in any selling activity: *time and information* – with an emphasis on information.

Whether a buyer or seller, the one who has the most information and who is under the least time pressure will always have the advantage. In this way, time and information can be your greatest ally or your biggest weakness in any negotiation. And, the only way to make both of them your friends is simple to state but difficult to accomplish. It is done by active listening; meaning that you listen with all of your senses.

Time

Time is a factor that can work for you or against you. In general, adding time to the selling process is your enemy, as the longer it takes to move though the process, the greater likelihood there is for some unforeseen element to appear and scuttle your efforts. But, at the same time, forcing the sale to conform to your time constraints will often create sales resistance that wasn't there before.

Ideally, each individual and each sale has its own pace that both parties feel comfortable with.

If you are listening actively, the client will tell you precisely what time factors are important or unimportant to them. Pay close attention.

Information

On an equal level of importance, information (or the lack of) can also be friend or foe. In general, the more information you can acquire, the more likely you will be able to align your selling pace to the comfort of the customer, and bring the sale to a mutually beneficial close.

It's said, over and over, that a major element of success in selling is the ability to ask questions and listen attentively. I cannot emphasize this enough. The buyer will nearly *always tell you what their hot buttons are*; whether it is their painful areas, or what their real purposes are for buying, they will tell you.

They may not say the words exactly or openly, but they are always letting you know in subtle (and often not so subtle) ways, exactly what you need to do to close the sale.

But you MUST be listening, carefully and actively.

Consider this: When was the last time you *listened* yourself out of the deal?

This truism will carry the day in most circumstances: The best way to convince others is with your ears.

Research their market, their company, and the person by whatever means available. Listen to what they're not saying. Be constantly alert with your ears and eyes wide open to gather all the information you can get about any prospect or their company.

Assuming that you know best about time or information on the part of the potential customer is a deadly flaw in any sales process – as it is with any communication between people.

If you must assume something, you're better served to *assume that you don't know* and then ask questions and actively listen to what they say. Used appropriately, time and information can be your best friends and allies if you let them.

YOUR WORST ENEMY

Oscar Wilde, one of London's most popular playwrights in the early 1890's once said:

"If you want to tell people the truth, make them laugh, otherwise they'll kill you."

I wish I were better at using humor in my writing, because this article **contains more truth** than some people can easily digest.

But this also may be one of the most important articles I've ever written because it solves a problem that has plagued more sales people than ever imagined.

So, it's time to let the truth out of the bag and damn the consequences. Here is the dirty little secret that every salesperson knows – *but doesn't want to admit.*

Law: Force creates resistance.

It's a vicious circle: You, as a salesman, encounter resistance, so you resort to forcing the customer. This creates even more resistance from them, and even more force from you.

And who wins at this "force – resistance" game?

No one! It's a "zero-win" game - and one guaranteed to create a loss for both sides.

Overwhelming the customer with pushy, bullying methods in an attempt to intimidate, dominate and force the prospect into buying from you, **will never work.**

Such tactics **always create trouble** for you and bruised feelings for the customer. It's a trap that has ruined more careers than you can shake a stick at.

There is only way out of this mess: Don't do it in the first place. This is an essential truth of selling based on the natural law:

Law: Force creates resistance – your worst enemy to closing a sale.

What has happened is that you, *or some earlier person,* forced that customer into doing something they didn't want to do, now they have an *instant-resist button* that rears its ugly head at the slightest hint of being forced into something.

A crude example is this: A customer digs in their heels and feels you are moving too fast. You, having used up all your more subtle tools of persuasion, resort to shouting at the customer or client. This drives them further away and creates an effect that is the opposite of what you wanted. It is also an admission that you haven't done your homework.

It is an indication that you don't understand selling and you don't understand people. It's also a sure way to end up scuttling your sales stats and leave you wondering what happened.

Sometimes, such techniques are aptly called *crush selling, as they attempt to seal the deal by crushing the customer into submission.* By whatever name, the customer knows it when they see it. It's *an act of desperation;* a symptom which indicates that an earlier step in the sales process was skipped.

In selling, amateurs force - masters adjust and adapt.

Be kind to your prospect, they've already got enough to worry about without you adding to their burden. To them, especially if it's a large purchase, it's a bit like stepping in to *mare incognito* (uncharted waters).

Help them. Don't try to force-feed them. Products and services are not sold; they're bought (willingly).

Prospects will buy when they see a *personal benefit* for themselves; not when it is being *pushed* down their throat.

Finally, if you have developed the (bad) habit of forcing customers, I have two words that will cure this habit instantly: STOP IT.

That is all there is to it. Just stop it. Now! The faster you stop it, the sooner you'll begin to develop habits that the customer agrees with. And isn't this what you're looking for anyway?

So, just don't force the customer again. Ever.

If for no other reason, it's very unprofessional; it is also just bad manners.

Instead, do it the easy way. Help the customer get what they want and they'll do the same for you.

YOUR BEST FRIEND

Who is your best friend? Is it your mom, your dad, siblings, wife, husband, children, or some other relatives? Or is it something closer to home, like your body, your mind, good looks or charm, your family, health, wealth, or your career?

Jazz trumpet legend, Miles Davis, said something that might give us the answer:

"Sometimes you have to play a long time to be able to play like yourself."

Intuitively, he knew something we all need to remember: **Your best friend is (or should be) you.**

Being you, and being a friend to yourself is *the most powerful asset you can possess.* It's what makes you stand out from all the rest; it's what makes you unique.

It's also the single most important and recognized path to success and happiness in any field. Being yourself is recognizing you, as an individual, with all your weaknesses and strengths. It means having the courage to express yourself as you really are and being comfortable with doing so. Many others agree:

From acclaimed best-selling author, e. cummings:

"It takes courage to grow up and become who you really are."

And from Steve Jobs:

"Your time is limited; so don't waste it living someone else's life."

Also a couple more:

"It took me a long time and much painful boomeranging of my expecta-tions to achieve a realization everyone else appears to have been born with: that I am nobody but myself." - Ralph Ellison

"The most important kind of freedom, is to be what you really are." - Jim Morrison

And finally, one of my favorites, which came from an epitaph on a grave marker in an old cemetery outside Tombstone, Arizona.

"Be who you is, cuz, if you be what you ain't, then you ain't what you is."

I couldn't have said it any better.

WINNING SKILLS AND ATTRIBUTES

Why do some salespeople seem effortlessly successful? What motivates them? What is the secret that makes them different from other professionals?

And most importantly, where do I get in line for my ticket to the *winner's circle*?

To enter the winner's circle, there are four winning sales attributes and six winning sales skills that must be part of your "sales DNA." These factors provide a bedrock foundation needed to make it in this profession.

What are *sales attributes*? They are qualities, personality, or characteristic traits that are either innate or have been learned. What this essay presents is a fact-based analysis of the most important attributes that all consistent winners have in common. So, if this is of interest to you, let's cut to the chase, set the niceties aside, look at the data and figure out what you need to know and how you can apply it.

The research
This information comes from thousands of hours of research, study and personal interface with salespeople in a variety of different sales positions in businesses of all sizes.

I discovered (not really a big surprise) that the consistent winners *never rely on sales tricks, fads or fashion methods du jour.*

Instead, the real source of the winners' success was based on the *bedrock fundamental principles and natural laws* underlying all sales and selling.

Also, lying far beneath the surface, are deeply rooted personality traits and skills acquired from *hard-won experience.*

This gives them a solid foundation to ride out the rough seas and to take advantage of good times to come. Now, lets look at some of the attributes of winners.

Four Winning Sales Attributes

1. Goal Orientation

Salespeople are motivated by money and orientated to this goal. But don't mistake this motivating factor as an insatiable, self-indulgent, materialistic greed.

Rather, they often gravitate to this profession because of the clear measures of success used in this environment. *You close the deal, you get paid.*

It's like the old "chicken or feathers" analogy. Sales = you eat chicken. No sales = you eat feathers. Clear and simple. Sales effectiveness is specifically measured and rewarded in financial terms, understood by all.

But, what is even more important is that he or she maintains maximum personal control of this measurement and reward system.

Salespeople are competitive and have a burning desire to win, although not necessarily to vanquish or to dominate peers.

The Hidden Reason

This reason may have never been clearly stated before; so give this your close attention, it's that important. Here it is: All winners are driven by this unsuspected internal element:

Winners are in constant competition with themselves.

Internal targets are decided on and set by themselves. They do not require external supervision. They are seeking to be better than their previous best.

This concept applies to all areas and efforts toward mastery and excellence as this quote illustrates:

"I'm in competition with myself. I just want to be able to play better tomorrow than I did today." - James Moody, American jazz master.

Money is only one way to keep score in the game and it is not necessarily the end goal. They're playing to win a game they have set up with themselves.

Often, they already are making more money than necessary to survive very comfortably by most standards. But that's not the point. Can they do better than they did last time? Can they beat their own personal best score? Can they outdo themselves?

These are the goals that are at stake in this game. More than anything else, this powerful need and *desire to master and excel* supplies the emotional, physical and mental energy and determination that motivates them to succeed.

Their demonstration of competence along these lines is what ultimately influences their morale, sense of worth and fulfillment for better or worse.

2. Recognition

A close second to goal orientation is responsiveness to recognition. Acceptable recognition may come in many forms: Titles and labels, formal performance recognition programs like "President's Club", "Sales Exec of the Year," etc., are examples of such programs.

Recognition is a strong motivator and many salespeople thrive on this, so the reward to the company in terms of increased sales cannot be ignored. Sometimes, just the casual acknowledgment from their peers is all that is needed to know that their contributions and successes are recognized. Whatever form it takes, this important element must not be ignored.

3. Responsibility For Others

Along with thinking of themselves as entrepreneurs, top salespeople often accept responsibility for everything in their environment, even including things over which they have no direct control. They really do care about their customers.

They often feel that they represent the entire company to their customers and position themselves as a virtual proxy for senior management.

This factor often translates into demands for greater quality and performance that can be harnessed to help the entire company improve.

However, poorly performing or non-responsive company personnel or resources can cause salespeople far more anguish than any other factor in the company.

After all, this not only hits at their paycheck, but their sense of responsibility for their clients as well.

This natural assumption of responsibility is a characteristic and quality that should be carefully nurtured and strengthened.

4. Belief In Self

Ultimately, most effective salespeople possess an abiding belief in themselves. This confidence is passionately felt and is contagious.

It can inspire similar feeling in others around you as well as in the customer, opening the door for a sale where one may not have existed previously.

Often the customer only needs to trust that you believe passionately that you deliver what you promise.

And this alone is sometimes all that is required to close the deal. The sales environment, more than any company function, thrusts people into situations requiring a high degree of personal confidence, belief, and intensity. For they are often placed in situations that *expose their weaknesses* when in the spotlight of a sales presentation.

Sales managers and trainers must, at times, provide correction and change.

But at the same time, be careful not to undermine the self-confidence and beliefs of individual salesmen or women. For we are a *delicate breed,* in spite of our outward bravado.

When management allows salespeople's core beliefs to be threatened, performance suffers; salespeople cannot survive in such an environment.

If management respects the salespeople's belief in themselves and the intensity with which it is felt, it becomes a path *to motivate and drive people to higher levels of performance*, which helps everyone in the company.

These four winning attributes are the vital components of the winning salesperson.

But there is more to this story. There is such a thing as the *skill* of salesmanship, quite in addition to attributes.

This skill is the application of the attributes described above, when applied to the real world of preparation, appointments, clients, presentations, objections, reaching an understanding and mutual benefit, closing and sealing the deal.

In addition to the four winning attributes above, the following six winning skill sets provide the combination necessary for entry to the winner's circle.

The skills required to consistently win at the sales game are as follows.

Six Winning Sales Skills

1. **Knowledge** is required to understand selling and to be able to work with others in the field. Selling cannot be reduced to a mechanical, rote procedure. It is a skill that draws from art and science and is a combination of the best of each field. It is also needed to handle both failures and successes.

2. **Efficiency** is the ability to perform with a minimum of effort for maximum result. It implies the ability to perform a task with fluency, smoothness, and grace. Since the most efficient form is also the most effective, the skill of efficiency is the bedrock upon which all other skills are based. Without efficiency in your sales form, being encumbered by force and effort will compromise the message you are seeking to convey.

3. **Automaticity** is the ability to perform without conscious aware-ness, mental effort, or monitoring. Without a doubt, it is one of the more important components of skill, for without it, we would be enmeshed in having to monitor the actions we take for granted.

4. **Timing** is the ability to do something at the proper moment in the proper sequence. This component contains all the elements of efficiency but contains the additional factor of being able to do a thing precisely when it is required. This allows us to coordinate our actions with others to achieve the desired results. Without it, efficiency is lost and the results are inconsistent.

5. **Adaptability** is the ability to perform under diverse or adverse conditions or circumstances. If you are not able to cope with the changing environmental factors involved with top-selling oppor-tunities, high-level performance will not be possible.

6. **Practice** is based on self-discipline. It is the time-honored route to skill retention and mastery. Bad habits are easy to acquire and hard to get rid of. So, while you practice, avail yourself of good, positive evaluation and/or correction from a trusted professional and you'll develop winning patterns.

Note that the six points above are in addition to the qualities understood to be essential to the skills of any salesperson: friendliness, self-discipline, initiative, and persistence. And also, the natural laws of selling apply from the simplest, one-on-one selling situation to the most complex, multilayered corporate sales environment and everything in between.

You cannot properly utilize a skill until you have mastered it. And mastery of anything requires dedicated focus and practiced repetition of the fundamentals.

If you're only halfway there in your skill level, this means that 50% of what you're doing is working for you, and 50% against you. You're wasting time and effort due to the lack of mastery in the basics, creating more problems than you solve.

Skill refinement offers entry into the level of sales mastery and is only attained from protracted practice. Bottom of Form

Advanced techniques are not skills that replace a more rudimentary skill. Advanced skills result from a *refinement and coordination* of the basics.

Advanced skills involve utilizing the same basic skill sets as the beginner, but they are developed for use at a much higher level of sophistication, ease and efficiency.

Don't try to rush to the advanced stage and neglect the basics. Sales excellence is built upon the essential truths. Master one level then move to the next. Then integrate both levels. When you've sufficiently mastered the basics, the more sophisticated skills become accessible.

For any who aspire to achieve excellence in selling, learn and apply the basics for *therein lies the magic.*

Excellence will appear unbidden upon mastery of the fundamentals.

Law: Excellence is based on the mastery of fundamentals, not the accumulation of techniques.

SALES MAXIMS FOR LIFE

L et's assume you've only got five minutes to jump-start your day with a high-octane boost of inspiration.

Carefully read a couple of these sales maxims for life with your morning coffee and I guarantee that you will find something to rapid-launch a successful day.

1. Find something you have in common with the prospect before you start selling.

2. Slow down and listen. It's the only way to connect with people.

3. Poor salespeople talk. Average salespeople listen. Top salespeople listen and tell a story.

4. If your attention is on the customer, you won't have time to be nervous, anxious or self-conscious.

5. The end result of worry and doubt is only more doubt and more worry.

6. All things being equal, people would rather buy from their friends. All things not being equal, people would still rather buy from their friends.

7. If you don't like or believe in yourself, why should anyone else?

8. Don't let the economic whip be your only motivation for selling.

9. Don't go to step three before you've fully completed step two.

10. *Selling is a contact sport.* If you're not in contact with people, you will sell nothing.

11. *Attention follows attention.* If you're worried only about your commission, don't be surprised when the prospect comes up with money concerns of their own.

12. If you want to be more interesting, be interested.

13. The key to opening a selling opportunity: Capture attention – *excite* imagination.

14. The "Four C's" of selling: Contact, Communicate, Connect, and Close.

15. Don't focus on *the close* - focus on the person.

16. People love to own, they don't like to buy. Sell the dream, not the product.

17. To make happy customers: Under-promise and over-deliver.

18. If you say it, it's *doubtful*. If they say it, *it's true*.

19. A *motionless salesperson* creates nothing. *Emotion creates motion.*

20. If the client can't see you as a solution, *you're the problem*. Don't keep selling to people that already have a solution.

21. People buy emotionally then justify it logically.

22. When you're closing, stop selling - unless you're trying to *talk them out of the sale.*

23. Market to people. *Sell to the individual.*

24. Telling people only what they want to hear helps no one but you.

25. If you're doing all the talking, you'll end up knowing nothing more than you started with.

26. Logic makes people *think*. Emotion makes people *act!*

27. If they don't understand it, they won't believe it. If they don't believe it, they won't feel it. If they don't feel it, *they won't buy it.*

28. Getting angry with the client is the most obvious sign that you have lost control of the situation.

29. Clients don't always know what they want – but they always know what they don't.

30. No salesperson has ever *listened* themselves out of a sale, but they commonly *talk* themselves out of one.

31. Honesty is in scant supply. To stand out from the crowd, tell the truth.

32. Difficulty at any step in the sales process means you skipped an earlier step

33. If an *indifferent* or obsessively agreeable customer never comes up with an objection, you are not going to close the sale.

34. The key to closing is when the prospect can see a *personal benefit in what you're offering.*

35. Anything is considered valuable, to a degree, *if someone wants it.* Your task is to nurture the desire created by marketing and advertising and turn it into a sale.

36. Your most valuable asset is your ability to observe.

37. You'll never get the order *you don't ask for.*

38. The customer's *motivation* for giving you money is rarely because you're broke – *unless her name is "Mom."*

39. In sales, *"conventional wisdom"* is usually neither.

40. Make clients **feel** something and you create a timeless, indelible impression.

41. Logic tells. Stories sell.

42. The prospect will begin to believe you're important once you *recognize that they are.*

43. Don't tell them you can solve their problems *before they recognize* there is a one.

44. Don't guarantee results for areas you can't directly control.

45. If they ask you what time it is – *don't tell them how to build a watch.*

46. Don't start talking until they start listening - and stop talking before they quit listening.

47. If the solution doesn't work in spite of everything, you've got the *wrong problem* or the *wrong solution.*

48. If you don't like or trust yourself, neither will they.

49. *First rule* of selling: Just show up. *Second rule* of selling: Don't tell everything you know.

50. You're in the **people** business - helping one individual at a time.

Note: First published in "My Success Company" under my nom de plume, Jacob Wright

.

THE END

APPENDIX

My grandfather, Seth B. Jacobs, author, editor, owner/operator of The Brighton Argus newspaper for 40 years, wrote the following essay on his 70th birthday in 1940.

RECIPE FOR LONGEVITY, HEALTH, AND HAPPINESS

Think only pure thoughts.

Look for the sunshine – ignore the shadows.

Think of others – forget self.

Don't complain.

Appreciate what is done for you.

Train your disposition to be cheerful.

Be temperate – especially in eating.

Don't be stingy with praise.

Find the good points in others, and tell them.

Make people like you; say ill of not one; either GOOD, or nothing.

Don't be afraid of exercise or fresh air.

Walk from the hips; chin up, breast out.

A bit of frivolity won't hurt you.

By Seth B. Jacobs

Daniel Jacobs, author

Index

www.ingramcontent.com/pod-product-compliance
Lightning Source LLC
Chambersburg PA
CBHW060419200326
41518CB00009B/1418